How to
Master

FINANCE

TERRY GASKING

How to
Master
FINANCE

A NO-NONSENSE GUIDE TO
UNDERSTANDING BUSINESS ACCOUNTS

**KOGAN
PAGE**

To Jill
and all the dogs that have shared our life

First published in 1991 by Business Books Limited
First published by Kogan Page Limited in 1999

Kogan Page Limited
120 Pentonville Road
London N1 9JN

© Terry Gasking, 1991, 1999

British Library Cataloguing in Publication Data

A CIP record for this book is available from the British Library.

ISBN 0 7494 3052 4

Typeset by Jean Cussons Typesetting, Diss, Norfolk
Printed and bound by Clays Ltd, St Ives plc

Contents

About the author, Terry Gasking FCCA. MIMIS. MIMgt. FRSA

Terry has worked in a variety of trades and industries as a highly successful financial consultant. He has lectured on finance at the University of Buckingham and spent a number of years as an Associated Lecturer at Ashridge Management College. For the past decade he has specialized on working with companies in the design and the implementation of in-house cash management programmes.

He has worked closely with non-accountants and non-financial managers and has helped them through many of the areas in finance that have puzzled them. He has found that by stripping away the buzzwords and mystique, the non-financial managers can understand the key elements of finance and can often implement them with exceptional clarity and focus.

This book therefore sets out to help the non-accountant, the student, and the non-financial manager to master finance.

The author is a widely travelled and is a well-respected consultant in cash and profits management. He enjoys working in companies from different trades and in different parts of the world and has a remarkable success rate in a whole variety of companies from three continents of the world.

His hobbies are golf, gardening, walking his dogs, walking in the hills (he recently walked across Scotland along the Great Glen in three days), and in recent years he has started to write books.

Terry is a very happy person.

Introduction

This book is for the non-accounting manager, the individual business person, and the student. It is written to help the reader who wants to understand finance without getting too bogged down in technical details, terms, and jargon.

Since the first edition the author has been greeted by many people in many parts of the world who report that it has achieved just that goal. It has helped them understand the subject and enabled them to talk to, and in some cases even understand, their accountant. They have been very kind in their comments. It has also been used as a core text for Business Studies and Introduction to Accounting and Finance at a number of business schools and colleges.

This second edition brings *How to Master Finance* up-to-date and hopes to guide the reader to the chapters and style of presentation they prefer.

The odd-numbered chapters of the book have been designed to give the reader a reasonably 'easy read'. So, if you move from Chapter 1 directly to Chapter 3, then 5, followed by 7, you have most of the basic knowledge you need to 'master finance' described in a manner that is easy to follow and understand.

The even-numbered chapters have been designed to cover some of the more technical details of financial documents and each elaborates on the subject of the previous chapter. Therefore, by reading the whole book, the reader covers the subject easily and gains a reasonable technical understanding.

The design of this book thus allows you the reader to decide how much knowledge you need and gives you the ability to read through the appropriate chapters either in 'easy read' style, or in more technical detail – or both.

Working with managers at all levels, over a period of some thirty years, has convinced me that the subject most non-accounting managers dislike, even fear, is finance. Certainly it is the one that causes them the most frustration.

Yet finance should be so *easy*!

Most of us manage our own household expenses quite reasonably. We pay our bills and make regular payments on our mortgage and other monthly charges. We balance our outgoings against our income, occasionally using a bank overdraft as a buffer when heavy expenditure comes in. We negotiate finance for ourselves when we enter into a loan agreement for extra cash to buy another car, or extend the house and so on. However, when we get into business, 90 per cent of us lose that basic common sense and manage finance poorly (sometimes very poorly).

Why is it that so many non-accounting managers find business finance so difficult? It is, I am sure, partly due to the mystique and confusion created by the terms and expressions used by the accountancy profession. In the late 1990s, the pendulum of power within a great number of companies swung towards accountants, and they have since shown that they will not easily release it. But accountants urgently need to learn communication skills if the businesses they work for are to perform to their full potential. In the twenty-first century, students and non-accountants can no longer evade their own responsibility to understand and master finance.

The accounting profession has a great deal to offer the business world, but it will achieve only a fraction of what is possible if the barriers that accountants have built around accounts are not removed. Barriers of terms and jargon and barriers of techniques. Although some techniques are unquestionably correct and in the best interest of the company, others might cause concern if the non-accountants really understood what was being perpetuated on their behalf.

How to Master Finance is produced to help to fill the void that exists between the non-accountant managers and the finance specialists. It will guide you in an interesting and invigorating way through the world of finance, and provide you with a reference book to consult whenever you need to.

If you are an absolute beginner or just reading this book out of general interest, then you will find it easier to read the odd-numbered chapters first as these provide necessary basic information. If you are an experienced manager with a reasonable grasp of the subject, but you require more detailed information, then read it straight through. An experienced manager who just needs his or her information 'topped-up' can concentrate on the even-numbered chapters for a reference base. A manager in a hurry for the relevant information can obtain instant answers from the even-numbered chapters and from the glossary that provides an instant reference and a pointer to the relevant part of the text.

I hope the simple no-nonsense approach of this book on finance helps to inform and advise and fill some of those vital gaps that may have been subconsciously troubling you over the years.

The explanations of financial terms and expressions are based on my own experiences over a period of 30 years and are specifically aimed at the non-accountant and student. They should not be taken as legal definitions. The views expressed are my own and are not to be taken as representing those of any accountancy association, training establishment, or any other body or institution, professional or otherwise. They are expressed to provide an understanding of finance as it is actually practised.

1

What are you worth?

Many managers have entered general management after having been excellent functional managers in the areas of production, sales, administration and so on. Some have taken a business studies course but many have learnt finance from the snippets they have picked up along the way. Some have been on one of the multitude of management courses on finance, such as Finance for Non-Financial Managers.

In almost every case, at all levels of non-financial management, there is a lack of understanding of finance, and this often stems from a poor understanding of the basic documents, the foundations from which accountants work. Understand what the main three accounting documents (balance sheet, profit and loss account and cash flow statement) are trying to tell you and you begin to get a feel of how to master finance. It is, therefore, from this point that we start.

If you were asked what you, personally, were worth, how would you answer?

One way could be to look at all the virtues you possess and answer with statements about the power of your personality, or your ability to think clearly in critical situations. You might take a slightly more mercenary approach and talk about your earning capacity or your ability to generate wealth. All these virtues are admirable and they may well reflect the way you value the attributes of other people, but from a financial point of view a more tangible method of assessment is necessary.

The virtues described in the previous paragraph may well be

those that you employ successfully in your work, and thus the keys to the type of income you can secure. The problems arise when one tries to put a value on these virtues.

How much is the power of your personality worth in pounds, dollars or yen? Is it worth £1, £10, or £100, or £1,000, £1 million or more? Accountants begin to run into difficulties with such questions and, with few exceptions, they like to account for the more tangible things in life. Possessions, for instance, are much easier to value.

Maybe it would make sense to look at the material items of your life and express your net worth in terms of your possessions. You could add up everything you own and then deduct any money you *owe* from the total value of those items and arrive at one way of revealing your worth.

If we follow this approach, and you are a house owner, then your statement of worth might well start with the value of that house:

House	£100,000

(It is interesting to note that when I have taken managers through this exercise at management college and at seminars around the world, they almost always select the current market value of their houses rather than some other criterion such as the price originally paid. For the moment it doesn't matter what method is used to value your house; value it by whatever method you feel is reasonable and fair.)

The next stage is the value of the contents of the house. There is often some doubt as to whether to value the contents at their original cost or at replacement value. You should choose for yourself the appropriate value in your own particular case. So, for example:

Contents	£16,000

Many managers drive a company car but, obviously, it should not be included in a personal statement of possessions as it is owned by the company. However, you should list any vehicles owned personally, by you or your spouse:

Vehicles	£8,000

What else might you own? Include any cash you might have in the bank or in the building society:

Cash	£1,750

Also list any salary that might be due for the days since your last pay day:

Salary outstanding	£1,250

It may be that you also possess some shares:

Shares	£700

In addition, you may have some life assurance or endowment policies; where this is the case, most managers seem to elect to value them at surrender (cash-in) value. However, they are often worth a lot more at maturity and we need to know how they have been valued. One of the ways of revealing this is simply to add the date of the valuation to the document. As of today's date, and assuming you are still alive, then the life insurance clearly has not yet reached maturity, so you have used the surrender value:

Insurances	£4,440

If you make out your own list of everything you own under similar headings to those above and below, you might enhance the benefits you receive from this book and become better equipped to master finance.

If you follow the author's suggestion, then your list of the things you own might look a little like this:

All that we OWN as at 30 September 20XX	
	£
House	100,000
Contents	16,000
Vehicles	8,000
Cash	1,750
Salary outstanding	1,250
Investments	
Shares	700
Insurances	4,440
Total Owned	£132,140

Having made out a list of all you own, you now need to deduct all you owe:

All that we OWE as at 30 September 20XX	
	£
Mortgage	60,000
Car Loan outstanding	2,000
Bills to pay (inc. credit cards)	2,300
Bank Overdraft	5,220

and so on.

This list can be set out in a way that is both neater and easier to read:

Our Worth as at 30 September 20XX		
	£	£
All that we own		
House	100,000	
Contents	16,000	
Vehicles	8,000	
Cash	1,750	
Salary outstanding	1,250	127,000
Investments		
Shares	700	
Insurances	4,440	5,140
Total owned		**£132,140**
All that we owe		
Mortgage	60,000	
Car Loan outstanding	2,000	
Bills to pay (inc. credit cards)	2,300	
Bank overdraft	5,220	
Total owed		£69,520
Net worth		**£62,620**

The net worth is calculated as being the total we own minus the total we owe (£132,140 – £69,520).

I have set out the a list of some of the things we might own and some of the things we might owe but the reader would gain a great deal from setting out their own statement of worth.

It can be seen that from this summary of net worth there are items that fall naturally into groups. The first section consists of items that have been bought to be used for some time ahead (certainly for longer than 12 months). We are going to call these *long-term assets*. The term assets is used to mean items that we own and that have a monetary value.

The second section contains items which belong to us but that we expect to change on a short-term basis (often daily but certainly within the next 12 months). These are referred to as *short-term assets*.

The third section contains investments of one kind or another and as we own them, and they have a monetary value, they must be listed among our assets. They are probably long-term but, as we might be tempted to cash them in if we need the cash, we are going to place them somewhere between the long-term and the short-term assets. We will continue to call them *investments*.

When we look at the things we owe, we again see an almost natural break between the debts we must pay very shortly (payable or could be called back by the lender within 12 months), and those that we have borrowed over a longer term. Again, we shall use short-term and long-term, but this time we shall call them liabilities to distinguish them as *things we owe that have a monetary value*.

We can now re-write our statement of net worth using different titles:

Statement of Net Worth as at 30 September 20XX

	£	£
LONG-TERM ASSETS		
House	100,000	
Contents	16,000	
Vehicles	8,000	124,000
INVESTMENTS		
Shares	700	
Insurances	4,440	5,140
SHORT-TERM ASSETS		
Salary outstanding	1,250	
Cash	1,750	3,000
Total ASSET VALUE		£132,140
SHORT-TERM LIABILITIES		
Bills to pay	2,300	
Bank overdraft	5,220	7,520

LONG-TERM LIABILITIES		
Car loan outstanding	2,000	
Mortgage	60,000	62,000
TOTAL LIABILITIES		**£69,520**
Net ASSET VALUE (net worth)		**£62,620**
(£132,140 owned – £69,520 owed)		

For the reader who is familiar with company accounts, it will be obvious that the statement of net worth we have produced above is similar to the document more usually called a *balance sheet* when produced for a business.

This gives rise to a definition of a balance sheet that many non-accounting managers have found a great help in unravelling the mysteries of finance:

> **A balance sheet**
> is merely the listing of
> **everything we OWN**
> less
> **everything we OWE.**

The only major difference between a company balance sheet and the one we have produced for ourselves, is the fact that we also show in the company balance sheet the *shareholders' funds*. The shareholders are the owners of a company and the people who originally provided funds used to buy the assets and build the company, ie in the above example they effectively supplied £62,620 of finance over the years.

Thus a company balance sheet would look something like the following (NB some companies' management reports show amounts owing in parentheses; however, they are seldom used in published accounts and reports and so have not been used here):

BALANCE SHEET of AB Ltd as at 30 September 20XX

	£	£
LONG-TERM ASSETS		
Land and buildings	100,000	
Plant and equipment	16,000	
Vehicles	8,000	124,000
INVESTMENTS		
Shares	700	
Insurances	4,440	5,140
SHORT-TERM ASSETS		
Debtors	1,250	
Cash	1,750	3,000
Total ASSET VALUE		**£132,140**
SHORT-TERM LIABILITIES		
Creditors	2,300	
Bank overdraft	5,220	7,520
Total Assets less Short-Term Liabilities		**£124,620**
LONG-TERM LIABILITIES		
Loans	2,000	
Mortgage	60,000	62,000
Net ASSET VALUE (Net Worth)		**£62,620**
Financed by:		
SHAREHOLDERS' FUNDS		
Ordinary Shares	10,000	
Capital reserve	20,000	
Revenue reserve	32,620	
TOTAL Shareholders' Funds		**£62,620**

I suggested earlier that you might gain a great deal by completing your personal 'balance sheet' or 'statement of net worth', so why not fill in the appropriate amounts in the list below? Don't get too hung up on exact values but use your best guess as to the 'market' value at today's date. Remember to head the document with today's date and then put the values you think are appropriate against each heading.

If you own a house and/or land then use what you think the market value will be. A lot of people wish to deduct the value of their mortgage but the mortgage is really a secured loan against the collateral of the house. The amount you show as a mortgage under 'owed' as a mortgage should be the amount outstanding at today's date (or rather the date of the statement). How much would it be if you tried to pay the whole sum back at the date of the statement? It should not include future interest payments. Take a moment or two to complete it:

The reader's worth as at	
	£
All that I own	
House and land	
Contents, furniture and fittings	
Vehicles	
Salary and any other monies owed to you	
Cash and money in short-term bank accounts	
Investments	
Other items of value	
Total owned	£
All that I owe	
Bills to pay (inc. credit cards)	
Bank overdraft	
Loans outstanding	
Mortgage	
Total we owe	£
Net worth (total owned – total owed)	£

To summarize the main points of this chapter:

- In almost every case, at all levels of non-financial management, there is a lack of understanding of finance, and this often stems from a poor understanding of the basic documents, the foundations from which accountants work.
- Understand what the main three accounting documents (balance sheet, profit and loss account and cash flow statement) are trying to tell you and you begin to get a feel of how to master finance.
- Tangible methods of assessment are necessary when calculating personal worth. Possessions, for instance, are much easier to value than personalities. Personal net worth can be calculated by adding up everything you own and then deducting any money that you owe.
- Among the things we own and the amounts we owe there are items that fall naturally into groups.
- The first section consists of items that have been bought to be used for some time ahead (certainly for longer than 12 months) – the long-term assets. The term assets is used to mean items that we own and that have a monetary value.
- The second section contains items which belong to us but which we expect to change on a short-term basis (often daily but certainly within the next 12 months) – short-term assets.
- The third section contains investments of one kind or another and as we own them, and they have a monetary value, they must be listed among our assets.
- When we look at the things we owe, we again see an almost natural break between the debts we must pay very shortly (payable or could be called back by the lender within 12 months) and those that we have borrowed over a longer term. We shall use short-term and long-term, but this time we shall call them liabilities to distinguish them as things we owe that have a monetary value.
- The statement of net worth is similar to the document more usually called a balance sheet when produced for a business.
- A balance sheet is merely the listing of everything we own less everything we owe.
- The major difference between a company balance sheet and the one we have produced for ourselves is the fact that we

also show in the company balance sheet the shareholders' funds.

● The shareholders are the owners of a company and the people who provided funds used to buy the assets and build the company.

Remember, the recommended way of reading this book is dependent on the needs of you the reader.

If you wish to get an overall view of finance, or if the subject is reasonably new to you, or if you are a little uncertain of the contents of the main financial documents, then I recommend that you skip Chapter 2 and proceed to Chapter 3.

If you are in a hurry for information on the balance sheet in particular and wish for a deeper study of it, then Chapter 2 is your recommended route. However, this more technical look at balance sheets can perhaps be more easily absorbed once the reader has the good general knowledge of finance that can be obtained from reading the odd-numbered chapters in this book first. Once the reader is comfortable with the principles behind the main accounting documents then the even numbered chapters can be easily absorbed.

2

The balance sheet

The secret of understanding finance is to keep it simple. Use common sense and enthusiasm. Don't over-complicate things.

In Chapter 1, we looked at just how easy it is to produce a balance sheet. If you are turning to this chapter from other parts of the book, or after some delay, it may be worth reading the summary at the end of Chapter 1 to remind yourself of its contents.

Providing you do not allow yourself to get caught up in arguments about the different ways of valuing assets then producing a balance sheet is easy. You merely list everything you own, give it a value, and then subtract the value of everything you owe and – hey presto – we have most of the constituent parts of a balance sheet.

As this is a book for managers as well as students, we have converted our list of assets and liabilities into a company balance sheet by adding the source from which our net worth originally came, viz. the shareholders' funds.

We shall now consider the balance sheet in some detail and ensure that you understand every item that appears on it. We will add another category of asset – *intangible assets* – and change and add a few more item headings along the way. These changes and additions will be explained as we go along.

If you have followed Chapter 1 successfully then the balance sheet shown below should not present you with too many problems.

I will talk about SSAPs (statements of standard accounting practices) along with international, European and national conventions and guidelines later, but at this stage be sure that you understand the base document fully before you move on. Remember, the secret is not to complicate things but to follow the simple explanations:

We will now examine each section of the balance sheet in more detail.

BALANCE SHEET of AB Ltd as at 30 September 20XX		
	£	£
FIXED ASSETS		
Land and buildings	100,000	
Plant and equipment	16,000	
Vehicles	8,000	124,000
INVESTMENTS		
Shares	700	
Insurances	4,440	5,140
INTANGIBLE ASSETS		
Intellectual rights	10,000	
Goodwill	8,000	18,000
CURRENT ASSETS		
Stock	20,000	
Debtors	1,250	
Cash	1,750	23,000
Total ASSET VALUE		£170,140
CURRENT LIABILITIES		
Creditors	2,300	
Bank overdraft	5,220	
Taxation	4,000	
Proposed dividends	1,000	12,520
Total assets less short-term liabilities		**£157,620**
LONG-TERM LIABILITIES		
Loans	2,000	
Debenture	10,000	
Mortgage	60,000	72,000
Net ASSET VALUE		**£85,620**
SHAREHOLDERS' FUNDS		
Ordinary shares	20,000	
Preference shares	8,000	
Capital reserve	20,000	
Revenue reserve	37,620	
TOTAL SHAREHOLDERS' FUNDS		**£85,620**

The title

A balance sheet is always drawn up as at a certain date (30 September 20XX). It is, therefore, only correct at that one precise moment. It is as though you were able to take a photograph of the business; it is correct only for the moment the shutter clicked. The following day, a business would have sold more items, received more cash from its debtors, owed more in wages, etc. Thus the amounts owned and the amounts owed would be different.

A balance sheet, because it is accurate at just one moment, is often said to be a 'snapshot of the company'. On its own, the balance sheet is not an accurate reflection of the strength of a company but more a reflection of the way the company has progressed over recent years.

For instance, the personal balance sheet that you produced in Chapter 1 might have shown that you had lived a diligent and sober life, carefully saving your money and investing wisely. On the other hand, you might have had quite a different lifestyle and spent your money as quickly as you earned it.

A balance sheet will therefore reflect financial diligence, or lack of it, over recent years and the idea of a snapshot at any one point needs to be tempered slightly by that fact.

Fixed assets

This term is almost guaranteed to cause confusion in the mind of a non-accounting manager or student. A much better title is the one we used in Chapter 1, long-term assets. However, fixed assets is the title that appears on most balance sheets, so we must examine just how 'fixed' these assets are.

Fixed assets contain a heading shown as 'Vehicles'. These obviously depart from the 'fixed' image as they not only hurtle all over the place but are also one of the easiest of the company's possessions to turn into cash. Take a vehicle to any of the many vehicle auction centres and you can turn it into cash immediately – and a darn sight quicker than many of the piles of stock you might have around the place.

Fixed assets are therefore clearly not labelled so because of their liquidity (how fast you can turn them into cash). There would seem to be very little reason for calling such items 'fixed', apart from tradition. Therefore, each time we use this term on a balance sheet, I ask you to think of the heading as long-term assets, ie we have invested in these items for the long-term benefit of the business and we do not expect to consume them within 12 months of purchase.

Spending on acquiring new fixed assets or on improving existing fixed assets is often called capital expenditure (sometimes shortened to CAPEX).

To nip another common confusion in the bud, expenditure on fixed assets (ie capital expenditure) has nothing whatever to do with fixed costs. (For a definition of fixed costs, see Glossary.)

Fixed assets, therefore, is a heading for:

- the tangible things we own;
- the tangible things that have a monetary value;
- the tangible things that we have purchased for long-term use in the business (longer than 12 months).

Fixed assets are normally separated into three major classes of investment for the long-term use of the business:

- Land and buildings;
- Plant and machinery;
- Vehicles.

The headings are not exclusive but they are the ones found on most balance sheets.

The value of the fixed assets is taken at cost (ie the actual sum of money paid) or at realization value (the money they could be sold for) or, sometimes, to some other formula. They are revalued on a regular basis and there is a move to have them revalued annually.

It would seem logical that if the balance sheet is drawn up on 30 September 20XX then the value of the fixed assets should be the value as at that date. The problem arises when we consider 'value': does it mean the value the asset would fetch if sold on that day or does it mean the value of the asset to the business on an on-going basis?

For example, in the balance sheet produced in Chapter 1, you included the contents of your house at your own valuation. When asked to do this, most people value their furniture, equipment and fittings at the price they paid for them less an amount to reflect the fair wear and tear the items have suffered since. This is reasonable, but the resultant value could be very different from the amount you would receive if you had suddenly to endure a house clearance (as anyone who has sold up after the death of an elderly relative will tell you).

In a clearance situation you might receive very little for all your contents, but on an on-going basis the contents are worth a great deal to you. If you had to replace them then it might cost you a great deal of money (probably a lot more than you have valued the existing contents).

There is, therefore, more than one way to value assets, and the way that is generally used by accountants is the going-concern basis. Assets are traditionally valued not on a clearance basis, or at market values, but at the value to the business presuming that the business is going to continue trading for many years ahead.

The contents of your home would thus be valued at the price you paid less an amount to reflect the wear and tear; the fixed assets of a business would follow the same principles. (I will discuss the reasons for re-valuing assets later in this chapter.)

Land and buildings

This is a fairly self-explanatory heading. It contains the value of all the land and buildings that the business owns and (in some cases) leases.

Leased land or buildings

Where a front-end premium has been paid (eg you pay £70,000 now for a seven-year occupancy of an office building), the company undoubtedly has an asset that should be included in its list of things owned (its balance sheet). There is a value attached to the unused portion of the lease.

If you were to draw up a balance sheet at the precise moment that your lease began, you would include a value of £70,000 under land and buildings. If you were to draw up a balance sheet in a year's time, you would only have six years left on the lease and you would have enjoyed one year's occupancy of the building.

The normal way of dealing with the diminishing value of a

lease would be by amortization – ie reducing the value left on the lease in a fair proportion to the length of the lease (in this example reducing it by a seventh for the year you've had). Therefore, £60,000 would be shown on next year's balance sheet as an asset in respect of this lease. The reduction in value (£10,000) would be deducted from that year's profit (more on this later when we look at profit and loss accounts). Thus over the period of the lease you gradually write off its full value until the lease is ended and no further value or occupation is left.

In addition to front-end premiums, the value of a profit rent (where the lease charge you are paying is less than the market value of the property) is often shown on the balance sheet under land and buildings.

Freehold land and property

Buildings and other fixed assets are treated in a similar way, in that they are 'written down' each year to reflect how much they have worn out over that year. However, another accounting idiosyncrasy comes in here, and we refer to this process not as amortization but as depreciation.

Depreciation

From the reader's point of view, the effect of depreciation on the assets of a business or person is pretty much the same as the amortization of a lease. When we depreciate an asset we attempt to write its value off over its lifetime.

Thus if you were to buy a car today for £10,000, in a year's time it would no longer be worth £10,000, even if you hardly ever used it. In your list of things you own (assets) you would put it at a lower value to reflect the fact that you had used up some of its original value. That is all we do when we depreciate an asset.

We don't put money on one side to replace business assets when they are fully worn out in five or ten years' time, any more than we keep a stash of cash somewhere earmarked solely to replace our personal car in four or five years' time. We use our money during those years for satisfying our needs, and probably give some thought in a year or two as to how to raise the money to replace the car when it gets towards the end of its useful life.

Exactly the same thinking applies to fixed assets and depreciation.

Plant and equipment

This title is usually given to the value of all the manufacturing plant owned, all the machinery, all the fixtures and fittings and all the office furniture and fittings.

The value of plant and equipment is usually stated as the original cost less depreciation. The details of new capital purchases (purchases of fixed assets) along with their depreciation is usually disclosed in a note attached to the balance sheet.

Plant and equipment is subject to regular revaluation in the same way as land and buildings.

Investments

This is the title given to monies or values invested outside the business. Into this category would go investments in the shares of other companies, in government securities, in overseas securities, etc. The investments are usually valued at cost or at market value, whichever is the lower.

If you have invested in other companies then the difficulty comes in putting a value on the shares. Do you use the stock market price as at that day?

It would seem sensible to do so as the title of the balance sheet gives the date. However, prices can change so abruptly, even during the course of the same day, so there is a danger that the value of the investments may be seriously overstated – they may drop dramatically. It is for this reason that the conservative or prudent accountant would probably value the investments at the lower of cost or realization value. (Realization value is often the same as market value where a drop in share price has taken place.)

Where investments have been valued prudently like this, you will often see a note attached to a balance sheet that reveals the directors' view of the real worth of the investments on the day the balance sheet was drawn up.

You may well ask why, if the balance sheet is dated 30 September 20XX, accountants play this charade. Why not show the value of investments on the balance sheet as at that date and so allow the reader to compare various balance sheets over the years and judge the investment skills of the directors on that basis?

I feel sure that this question would prompt a lengthy discourse among accountants eager to justify this action. But the plain logic is that if a balance sheet is dated 30 September 20XX then it should contain all the values at that date if it is to be truly meaningful, instead of necessitating a scurry through all the attached notes in order to obtain the information.

Generally, accountants have still to learn a great deal about communication skills (even though it could be argued that it should be the number one requirement) and the multitude of training courses on finance for the non-financial manager bear witness to this fact. Therefore, I am afraid that you must bear with this quaint little custom for the time being and dig around for the values as at the date of the balance sheet.

Intangible assets

Accountants have all sorts of difficulties in valuing intangible assets and with good reason: they are, after all, intangible.

There are a number of items that comprise intangible assets, and we will deal with goodwill first.

Goodwill

When someone buys a ready-made business that has been trading for a few years or more, the seller inevitably wants something for the company's goodwill. Goodwill is loosely described as the value of the client base that regularly buys from the business, or the value of the business's good name or reputation.

Undoubtedly some such value exists (as anyone who has formed a new company entirely from scratch will readily agree), but what is the value? How do you measure it?

There are many theories and all kinds of 'expert' companies that specialize in this area, but the value must at any time be fairly subjective. The value of goodwill will always be in the eyes of the beholder.

It's rather like the question in the opening chapter – what are you worth? If you tried to put a value on your skills, experience and personality, the resultant figure might be very different from the value put on you by another person, such as your employer, your bank manager or one of your friends. They will have their own criteria for measuring wealth and it is likely that each would come up with a different value. So it is with the value of goodwill to a business.

When selling a business, you not only have to take account of the differing ways of valuing the assets but you also have to take account of the value of the increased profits that the buyer can expect in future years. The value of these benefits will differ widely in the eyes of the interested parties and all the complex calculations in the world will not resolve the problem of establishing the real value of goodwill.

The only time we really know what goodwill is worth is the moment a deal to buy another business is completed. At that moment the buyer and the seller have agreed terms and thus defined the amount of goodwill that is included in the final payment.

Your balance sheet from Chapter 1 will serve as an example. This shows a net asset value (or net worth) of £62,620.

If I were to come along with a bid to 'take you over', you would be very likely to point out that you hadn't revalued all your assets for some time and that they might be worth more than is shown on your balance sheet.

You might also point out that, although your net asset value is only £62,620, you do in fact earn just over £15,000 per annum with every chance of future increases and I would thus get my money back in four years. You therefore feel that you are worth more than £62,620 and you push me for a higher figure and ask for £100,000.

I, on the other hand, point out that I feel that some of your assets may be overvalued and that you have forgotten to deduct your living costs from the £15,000, so it will take me much longer than four years to get my money back. Indeed, I would have to find you better-paid work to make my investment worthwhile. I offer you £50,000.

Let us suppose that we have been sufficiently impressed by each other's arguments to reassess our values and that eventually we agree a price of £80,000.

I have now bought your company (or in this case you) for £80,000 and have taken responsibility for clearing all your debts as well as owning all your assets. I thus add all your assets to the assets shown on my balance sheet and add your liabilities to those I was previously showing.

The result is that, after the takeover, the net asset value shown on my balance sheet (my net worth) has increased by a net £62,620, but my cash has gone down by the £80,000 I paid for you at the takeover.

I would be a fool to pay you £80,000 if your business was not worth that amount, so what I have paid for over and above the figures shown on the balance sheet must have been something intangible called 'goodwill'.

Your goodwill has therefore cost me £17,380 (the £80,000 I paid less the £62,620 your balance sheet stated as your net worth). If you had inserted this value for goodwill under intangible assets on your balance sheet, it would have brought the value of everything I bought up to the purchase price I paid.

So, your original balance sheet plus goodwill would give:

BALANCE SHEET of **AB LTD** as at 30 September 20XX		
LONG-TERM ASSETS		
House	100,000	
Plant and equipment	16,000	
Vehicle	8,000	124,000
INVESTMENTS		
Shares	700	
Insurances	4,440	5,140
INTANGIBLE ASSETS		
Goodwill		17,380
SHORT-TERM ASSETS		
Debtors	1,250	
Cash	1,750	3,000
Total ASSET VALUE		**£149,520**
SHORT-TERM LIABILITIES		
Creditors	2,300	
Bank overdraft	5,220	7,520
LONG-TERM LIABILITIES		
Loans	2,000	
Mortgage	60,000	62,000
Net ASSET VALUE (net worth)		**£80,000**

There is little point in changing your balance sheet in advance as we do not know what the exact value of goodwill is until the deal is made. (With regard to this, UK accountants thought of a lovely wheeze, which hoisted many on their own petards in the early 1990s, but they may well do the same again in 2010 and 2031. This will be discussed at the end of this chapter.)

We therefore tend to leave the seller's balance sheet as it was last published, making all the adjustments on the balance sheet of the purchasing company. My balance sheet would therefore absorb all your assets and liabilities (including the asset of goodwill at a value of £17,380) and the resultant £80,000 increase in my net asset value would be eradicated by a reduced cash holding of £80,000 to reflect the payment I made to you.

In other words, instead of possessing cash to the value of £80,000, I now possess all the assets and liabilities that were formerly owned by you with the addition of goodwill valued at £17,380. The various ways goodwill is subsequently treated in company accounts are dealt with later.

Brand values (what's in a name?)

A few years ago, a number of directors of leading companies began to feel uneasy that the balance sheets of their companies were understating their true worth by ignoring the inherent goodwill. The accountants argued against the inclusion of goodwill on the grounds discussed above, ie it is impossible to put an accurate value on goodwill unless an offer for the company has been made.

Most companies wish to remove goodwill from their balance sheet as fast as possible for reasons considered later. However, the exceptions really wish to boost their balance sheet values for reasons that usually include a defence against potential takeover – or to gain a better deal if they are selling out to a predator.

It seemed that a sort of unholy alliance took place and somebody astutely worked out that it would be legitimate to include a value for any outstanding brand names that the company owned.

There is undoubtedly considerable value in many brand names. All of us buy particular brands of products and we will look for those products on the shelves before any others. The value that can be attached to brand names was highlighted in one or two famous takeovers of the 1980s, and as a result many companies included brand values in their balance sheets.

How do you work out the value of a brand name? A few specialist companies will offer to do it for you for a fee, but you might try to do it for yourself. Compare two similar products, one with a well-known brand name and the other unknown, and work out the additional gross profit that results from the additional sales achieved by the branded product (it is preferable to use contribution rather than gross profit).

After much calculation and heart-searching you can come up with a figure for the value of brand names, though how much validity it has is open to question. However, there is a reasonably valid argument that the value should appear as an intangible asset and thus increase the value of the assets the company owns.

The only time we know whether the figure for brand values is accurate is when someone wishes to buy the company, or the brand, and agrees a price. In that way, it differs very little from goodwill. It could be argued that brand values are in fact included in goodwill and make up part of that additional value, for which people are prepared to pay you over and above the net asset value of your business. If that is so, why do we take so much trouble over brand values, intellectual property and other intangible assets when most companies in the UK fall over themselves to write goodwill out of the balance sheet?

Research and development (intellectual property)

Another intangible asset that is often seen on balance sheets goes under the name of intellectual property, which is often an upmarket name for research and development or the results thereof.

Research and development (R&D) can be treated in two quite different ways. The entire expenditure can be charged against the profits made in the year the expense was incurred, or expenditure on research and development may be 'capitalized' and shown on the balance sheet as an intangible asset.

When R&D is 'capitalized' what effectively happens is that the total cost of all the materials, labour and expenses that have been used during the year on R&D is kept in a separate account. Instead of charging this total against profits on the profit and loss account, it appears as an asset on the balance sheet, just as if you had spent that amount of money on some plant and equipment that you intend to use over the years ahead.

The key point here is the intention to benefit from the R&D expenditure over the years ahead.

The expenditure may occur now, but the benefit from R&D might not occur for a number of years – the time it takes to complete the development and market the end product successfully. In these circumstances R&D will often be capitalized to appear on the balance sheet and then be gradually written off over the lifetime of the product or service that was being developed, in much the same way as other assets are depreciated.

Take care, though. Much R&D is pure research and most of that will have no commercial value whatsoever. In these circumstances it would be prudent to write the entire amount off against profits as soon as possible and only capitalize the R&D that is going to result in a commercial product that will actually sell.

One of Britain's leading computer companies has made the mistake of capitalizing intellectual property only to find that, once fully developed, there was no market for its beautiful product. Development costs totalling over £1.5 million subsequently had to be written off the profit and loss account in the year when it was finally realized that there was no value to all the R&D undertaken on that product.

Current assets

Remember that current assets are really short-term assets (Chapter 1), ie the intention is that they should be held for as short a time as possible. If we are buying an asset of significant worth and expect to hold on to it for longer than a year then it is listed among plant and equipment as a fixed (long-term) asset. (The definition of significant worth will depend on the circumstances of the particular business.)

Current assets earn nothing, but they cost the business money. They only earn once they have been turned into saleable products or services and are sold on (and when payment has actually been received from the customer and has been paid into the business's bank account).

Most people trying to build a business need (or think they need) to borrow cash, particularly in their earlier years. Many must therefore go to their bank managers to secure a loan. Remember here that the subsequent 'negotiation' is generally stacked against you: the banks have the money; you need it. Over the years, the control the bankers have enjoyed has led to demands that balance sheets should be strong enough to ensure that the bankers' money is not at risk.

Bankers like the profit their charges and interest rates bring them, but they do not like taking risks. So, in order to 'minimize' the risk factor, most accountants are taught that the balance sheet should contain twice the value of current assets as it has in current liabilities.

To make matters worse, there is, or rather was, a school of thought stating that businesses should match their total current liabilities with debtors and cash/short-term deposits in their current assets. This splendid ratio (known as the 1:~1, or liquidity, ratio) allowed the bankers to enjoy a splendid income from your interest and charges with virtually no risk to them whatsoever.

The problem with the above two ratios (2:~1 and 1:~1) is that the business is tying up huge amounts of cash that earns nothing, which I do not see as being management in the best interest of the shareholders.

During the 1990s, I have worked with many companies where we have actually turned the working capital negative, ie total current liabilities became greater than total current assets. Nowadays we want current assets to be as low as possible commensurate with risk (the logic of this statement is explained in Chapter 10 where we look at performance ratios).

Stock (inventory)

When stock appears as a current asset, it refers to items we possess that will be made up into products or services for resale. It does not refer to, or have anything to do with, stocks and shares or any kind of borrowings or lendings.

A better name for stock is inventory, but in the UK, and in many published accounts throughout the world, the value of inventory is listed under the title of stock.

Valuing stock should be comparatively simple, but it can be a pantomime and I have heard managers refer to this item as 'the accountants' fiddle-factor'. I really can't answer that – I am sure that the reference was in jest!

Stock is usually valued at the lower of cost or realization value.

Cost is the price actually paid for the items when they were purchased.

Realization value is the lower of the values for which the stock can be purchased or sold. Where prices drop dramatically (as in the computer industry since the microchip went into production), it is often impossible to sell the stock at the price paid for it. In such instances the realization value, rather than the price you paid for it, would be used.

Valuing raw materials this way is fairly simple, but problems begin to appear when we think of 'work-in-progress' and 'finished stocks'.

Work-in-progress has incurred the cost of the raw material and the cost of the labour that has worked on it to date. In addition, it has picked up the cost of the space it has occupied in the factory, and a share of the overheads that the business has incurred while getting the raw material to its present stage of manufacture.

Where the stocks of the raw material are plentiful, and its price has been changing regularly, the accountant must decide how to charge the material out of stores and on to the job. There are several methods on which to base this decision. First, the basis that the first item received in the stores is the first to be issued (first in first out – FIFO). Second, that the last item received is the first item issued by stores (last in first out – LIFO). Third, that the average price of all relevant material is calculated and applied.

There are other charging methods, such as charging a standard price for each item as it moves through the factory, or setting a price at the beginning of the year and then updating it, say, quarterly.

All these different ways of valuing stock will give different results. It seems that by changing the method of stock valuation the accountant can dramatically influence the financial results. However, one of our principles as accountants is that if we do change the basis of stock valuation, we must carry a note on the accounts stating that this has occurred. The note to the accounts must also show the effect the change has had on that year's profits (how stock values affect profit will be seen in chapters 3 and 4).

Therefore, stock includes the value of:

● raw materials;
● work in progress;
● finished stocks.

Debtors and creditors

My experience is that up to 60 per cent of managers (senior, middle and junior) confuse debtors and creditors. Although this figure is reducing, thanks to improvements in managers' financial awareness, it remains sufficiently high to allow vital areas of control to go astray.

Part of the reason for this confusion comes from the names themselves. Many people feel that 'debtors' represents the people we are in debt to and creditors are people with whom we have credit. Alas, it is not so!

Another part of the reason for this confusion comes from the titles used on bank statements where money paid into the account is credited, while money going out of the account is debited.

The confusion is deepened by the fact that it is the 'credit controller' (who should be named debtor controller) who chases our customers for payment. So the customers must be creditors? Alas no!

Accountants use the terms debtors for customers and creditors for suppliers. As the job of the accountant is to communicate the accounts to other managers, there seems to be a strong argument in favour of a change to more easily understood titles. But accountants are traditionally a conservative lot and such change will probably have to be forced on them by the demands of the non-accounting managers!

Why can't customers' accounts be called customers' accounts? Why can't suppliers' accounts be called suppliers' accounts? Ah well, wishful thinking! Customers' accounts are called debtors. Suppliers' accounts are called creditors.

Debtors are: accounts receivables; customers' accounts; people who owe us money – *our* money is in *their* bank accounts.

Debtors, then, are our account customers who have had our goods and services but are still to pay us. They are therefore listed among our current assets as money we own but that is in our customers' hands. (Current as you hope to receive this cash within 12 months). The totals shown under debtors also include payments you might have made in advance to a recipient who must therefore owe us a service of some kind.

Creditors are: accounts payable; suppliers' accounts; people to whom we owe money – *their* money in *our* bank accounts.

As we shall see later, the effective control of debtors and creditors is crucial to any business, so it is imperative that you understand fully the meanings of these terms.

Cash

Cash usually includes the petty cash you hold in the business as well as monies in the business bank account or on short-term deposit. It is the stuff that pays the bills!

Now we have completed current assets we have finished listing everything the company owns that has a monetary value (ie we have listed all its assets). For example:

BALANCE SHEET of **AB LTD** as at 30 September 20XX		
	£	£
FIXED ASSETS		
Land and buildings	100,000	
Plant and equipment	16,000	
Vehicles	8,000	124,000
INVESTMENTS		
Shares	700	
Insurances	4,440	5,140
INTANGIBLE ASSETS		
Goodwill	17,380	
Intellectual property	30,000	47,380
CURRENT ASSETS		
Stock	20,000	
Debtors	1,250	
Cash	1,750	23,000
Total ASSET VALUE		**£199,520**

We can now start to list everything the business owes, just as we did in Chapter 1. For example:

CURRENT LIABILITIES		
Creditors	2,300	
Bank overdraft	5,220	7,520
LONG-TERM LIABILITIES		
Loans	2,000	
Mortgage	60,000	62,000

Accountants use the word liabilities on the balance sheet to signify an amount that the business owes to somebody or to some other company.

Current liabilities

This is the title given to the group of debts that could or must be paid within the short-term, ie within the next 12 months.

The debts we list under current liabilities include:

- creditors;
- bank overdraft;
- taxation;
- dividends (unpaid).

Creditors

Debtor and creditor control is so fundamental to the financial well-being of any company that it is imperative that you read the descriptions given above and study the page until you are happy that you will never mix them up.

Remember: creditors are: accounts payable; suppliers' accounts; people to whom we owe money – *their* money in *our* bank accounts.

Also listed under creditors are accruals. Accruals occur where we have had the benefit of goods or services but have not yet received or processed the invoice for them. An example might be the telephone. If we are halfway through a quarter when we draw up our balance sheet then there will have been many phone calls that we have made for which we have not received an invoice.

Where this occurs we make our best guess at the value of the services we have received (ie we make an accrual) and we include that cost in our profit and loss account. As we have not paid the supplier for an invoice we have not received, we also add that value to the amounts outstanding to our creditors (people to whom we owe money).

To be listed as a short-term liability (current liability) the debts should be payable within the next 12 months. Long-term debts are listed under precisely that title below.

Bank overdraft

Some bank overdrafts seem to continue for many years, so why

33

are these listed under short-term (current) liabilities? The answer is that a bank overdraft is really a temporary facility and if you read the small print you will usually find that the bank manager can recall it on demand if he or she should feel unsure of your ability to pay.

A bank overdraft, therefore, is recallable on demand and thus repayable within 12 months and listed as a current liability.

Taxation

A company can owe tax for a number of reasons. It could have collected VAT (value added tax – a type of sales tax) on its sales and this, less the VAT it has paid on its purchases, is payable to Customs and Excise, usually on a quarterly basis (NB business accounts are normally recorded with VAT excluded from the transactions).

If the company made profits last year, it will be taxed on those profits in accordance with Corporation Tax requirements. The profit is drawn up for the year and adjusted for capital allowances before the tax liability is known. The resultant liability is to be paid during the following year, hence the taxation that is owed in the following year's accounts is a short-term (current) liability.

Dividends

Dividends are the share of the company's profits that is to be paid out to the owners of the company (its shareholders). Usually an interim dividend is paid just after half the year is complete, and the final dividend is declared when the end-of-year results are known.

As all the profits belong to the shareholders, it is required that they vote to allow the directors to keep any of their money in the company to manage for the following year (although these days directors seem to keep an increasing amount of shareholders' profits for their own remuneration!). The dividend, therefore, must be ratified by the shareholders at the annual general meeting that is held some time after the year-end.

The current liabilities will therefore contain the amount of dividend that is proposed to be paid.

We have now listed the total assets and subtracted the short-term liabilities and this subtotal (total assets less current liabilities) is regarded as the amount of money that is actually tied up in the business. Everything on the balance sheet down to that level is usually in the control of its managers and directors, and it is the return that they achieve upon this value that is (or should be) the principal measure of the success of their management.

Total assets less current liabilities is therefore often referred to as the *capital employed*. The following example illustrates this:

BALANCE SHEET of AB LTD as at 30 September 20XX		
	£	£
FIXED ASSETS		
Land and buildings	100,000	
Plant and equipment	16,000	
Vehicles	8,000	124,000
INVESTMENTS		
Shares	700	
Insurances	4,440	5,140
INTANGIBLE ASSETS		
Goodwill	17,380	
Intellectual property	30,000	47,380
CURRENT ASSETS		
Stock	20,000	
Debtors	1,250	
Cash	1,750	23,000
Total ASSET VALUE		**£199,520**
Current liabilities		
Creditors	2,300	
Bank overdraft	5,220	
Taxation	1,250	
Dividends (unpaid)	2,000	10,770
Capital employed (total assets less current liabilities)		**£188,750**

We have now listed everything that the company owns that has a monetary value (the assets) plus the short-term borrowings (the current liabilities).

The only headings we have left on the balance sheet are: medium and long-term borrowings; shareholders' funds.

When a company wishes to raise funds to finance a new project (eg purchase new plant and equipment, conduct a new marketing campaign, undertake some R&D, fund new offices, etc) there is a limit to the number of places it can go to get the necessary finance.

It can approach the shareholders and ask them for some more money. The problem here is that nearly everyone I've met who owns shares in a company invariably holds them with the idea that the shares will make money for them. The shareholders only make money if the company makes a profit and only receive that money if the company pays a dividend, so if they supply a company with more of their money then it has to earn more profits. How much more?

In the late 1980s and early 1990s, the UK government decided to use interest rates to cure inflation and the base rate stayed at about 15 per cent. Banks make money by using the deposits of their customers (on which they pay interest at 2–3 per cent below the base rate). The banks lend that money at varying rates: 2–3 per cent above base to first-class 'blue-chip' companies; 5–6 per cent above to the less well-established companies; and at even higher rates to those unfortunates who desperately need the money to keep going or to finance the start-up of a project.

In the late 1980s and early 1990s it was possible to deposit cash in a number of quite safe havens outside the normal bank deposit accounts and receive 15–16 per cent on your money. That being the case, the shareholders are going to want considerably more than 16 per cent from their investment in your company, with all its inherent risks.

In the late twentieth century the bank rate fell to single figures and this eased the return required by businesses. However, they still needed to exceed 12 per cent return on the investments made in them by their shareholders.

If shareholders deposit their money in the bank, or somewhere similar, it can be retrieved at short notice. But if it is invested in shares in your company they must first sell their shares before they can get their money back, and the amount they receive will be subject to the whims of the stock market and its interpretation of your company's future profits.

How much interest would you want? Well, if you are about to put all your hard-earned money into a business, I suspect you would want considerably more than you can obtain from a bank, probably in excess of 15 per cent per annum.

Money from shareholders is therefore not cheap money as they will need a fair return from the risk they are taking in loosing control of their cash by investing in your business.

If we can't make 15 per cent or more on their investment then we have a problem as we still need to fund this new project. Perhaps we can borrow from the banks.

I find that bankers in the UK are a strange breed. They lend huge companies, and projects in developing countries, over-whelming amounts of cash with very little effective security, but if a small company wants to borrow then they will almost certainly require some sort of security (collateral). Usually they will insist on a charge over the assets of the company and some-times the private property of its directors as well. Therefore, in the event of the company being unable to meet the repayments or interest charges, the bank can seize the assets and the directors' properties as their own. It is usually somewhat difficult to carry on trading under these circumstances.

Borrowing from a bank, therefore, has more risks attached to it than money from the shareholders, but you can often get the cash for a few points less than the shareholders would expect.

Instead of borrowing from the bank it is possible to borrow from a whole host of people by way of a debenture or bonds. These can be structured in a variety of ways including an option to the company or the holder to convert the bond into shares in the company at some future time instead of getting their money back. If the price of the share at conversion is agreed at the time of borrowing the money then the company can tempt the lender to take a chance on the possibility of a capital gain on the share price.

There is a multitude of such borrowing instruments but here it is enough to realize that the purpose of them all is an attempt by the company to borrow money in the most attractive way possible.

A third way of raising money is to generate it from inside the company by selling the company's goods and services for more than the entire cost of making and providing them including all the support costs (interest payments on borrowed funds, taxation, etc).

Care must be taken with this third source as we have just loosely defined profit, and the profit of the company belongs to the shareholders. That is why they invest their cash in the company in the first place, so that they might enjoy the resultant profits.

Retained profits must therefore make the same amount of return as any additional funds for which you ask the shareholders, ie certainly more than that provided by the banks or other safe havens.

Sources of finance

The listing of long-term liabilities and shareholders' funds is often done under the heading of sources of finance as the following example illustrates:

LONG-TERM LIABILITIES		
Loans	2,000	
Bonds and debenture	10,000	
Mortgage	<u>60,000</u>	72,000
SHAREHOLDERS' FUNDS		
Ordinary shares	20,000	
Preference shares	8,000	
Capital reserve	50,000	
Revenue reserve	<u>38,750</u>	<u>116,750</u>
<u>Total</u>		<u>**£188,750**</u>

Long-term liabilities

Long-term liabilities are all the sources of finance as discussed in the last couple of pages, but they are borrowings, not shares. The lenders may have the right to convert their bonds or debentures into shares if those rights were given at the time of the lending but until such conversion takes place they remain lenders and not shareholders.

Where conversion or reversion rights exist (ie borrowings may be converted into shares) the accountants will normally show not only the earnings per share with the shareholding as it is now (before conversion) but will also attach a note to the accounts showing *fully diluted earnings* – where the earnings are divided by the number of shares that would have been issued had all the borrowings that are convertible, now or in the future, been converted into shares at the date of the balance sheet.

Long-term liabilities are often separated into two sections: medium-term (usually repayable in one to five years); long-term (repayable six or more years ahead).

A debt that the company owes is therefore listed according to the date of repayment. A 30-year mortgage might spend years 30 down to 6 being listed under long-term liabilities. Years 5, 4, 3, 2, 1 would be listed under medium-term liabilities, and in the last year it would be shown as a current liability.

In the most popular method of laying out the balance sheet the medium- and long-term liabilities are deducted from the total assets less current liabilities (the capital employed) to give a net asset value in a similar way to our example at the end of Chapter 1. The following gives an example:

Capital employed		£188,750
less LONG-TERM LIABILITIES		
Loans	2,000	
Bonds and debenture	10,000	
Mortgage	60,000	72,000
Net asset value		£116,750
SHAREHOLDERS' FUNDS		
Ordinary shares	20,000	
Preference shares	8,000	
Capital reserve	50,000	
Revenue reserve	38,750	
Total SHAREHOLDERS' FUNDS		£116,750

Shareholders' funds

Ordinary shares

Authorized @ £1	£50,000
Issued	£20,000

The holders of ordinary shares are usually referred to as the owners of the company. In the example shown above the company is authorized by its shareholders and by the Registrar of Companies to issue up to 50,000 shares, each of which having a nominal value of £1 (ie it is written on the share certificate that it is worth £1). However, it has not yet issued all 50,000 of them.

Once issued with a share, the shareholder in a publicly quoted company may be free to sell that share to someone who wishes, or can be encouraged, to buy it. As with all trading, the price at which the share changes hands depends upon the negotiations between the seller and the buyer. It will depend on how many other existing shareholders are trying to sell their shares at that time and how many people are wishing to buy.

Buying and selling shares follows many similar rules to those of your local fruit market, with the dealers doing the job of the barrow boy (there are a number of other similarities, too). They will fix their prices according to expected demand and supply of a particular share and then react to those same two pressures throughout each day.

The price at which a share changes hands after it has been issued may therefore have little to do with its nominal price, and may change dramatically each day. The published accounts do not usually report the 'current' stock market price and the value of the shares issued shown on the balance sheet is calculated by taking the number issued at the nominal price that is shown on the share certificate.

A new issue of shares (eg the company decides to issue some of those remaining 30,000 shares that are authorized but not yet issued) is often at a price nearer to the market price than the nominal value. The newly issued shares, however, carry the same rights to voting and profit as those previously issued (unless the company has a special class of ordinary share, such as a president's share or the government's golden share – as in the privatized BP and Jaguar share issues).

To illustrate the above, let us assume that the company is trading successfully and that there is a ready market for its shares at about £5 a share. It has decided to issue another 10,000 shares at £5 each.

The company will receive 10,000 times £5 in cash (so its cash listed under current assets on the balance sheet will increase by £50,000).

It has issued 10,000 ordinary shares, so its ordinary shares issue will increase by 10,000 @ £1 = £10,000.

The remaining £40,000 (£50,000 received in cash less the £10,000 shown as an increase in ordinary shares issued) is known as a share premium and is listed among the items reported as capital reserves.

For example:

SHAREHOLDERS' FUNDS		
Ordinary shares Authorized @ £1		£50,000
Issued	30,000	
Preference shares	8,000	
Capital reserve	90,000	
Revenue reserve	38,750	
TOTAL SHAREHOLDERS' FUNDS		**£166,750**

Note that, as a result of the issue of the additional shares, total shareholders' funds have increased by £50,000 to £166,750. This is balanced by the additional cash shown under current assets, which has increased by £50,000.

The capital reserve therefore contains share premiums, as discussed and illustrated above, and other capital profits, particularly any increase in valuation resulting from a revaluation of land and buildings.

Before the days of galloping property prices, many companies never bothered to revalue their assets and left them in the books at the price they originally paid, less any depreciation they had charged over the years. As they had no intention of selling the asset, it didn't make much sense to revalue. But then along came the asset-strippers, who managed to pick up many a company cheaply.

The asset-strippers didn't share the previous owners' romantic views of their business. They were not reluctant to close any part of it or to move it to leased premises, with the result that they were able to release all the property gains that had formerly been hidden in the balance sheet and enjoy the cash for themselves.

Nowadays it is deemed sensible to revalue regularly and reflect the value of the assets on the day the balance sheet is drawn up. Indeed, from the shareholder's point of view, or that of anyone dealing with the company, it makes complete sense for a balance sheet to contain all the values as at that date.

Let us assume that our company revalues each year. (I hear the cries of the senior managers and accountants cursing me for suggesting such a thing and thus making their return on capital employed look far worse.) If the result of revaluing is that you no longer make sufficient return on capital employed then the solution is to strip your assets. Sell the assets that fail to provide sufficient return and either reinvest that money in the areas of the business that give the return your shareholders require or give it back to the shareholders and let them invest it elsewhere.

In our latest set of accounts for AB Ltd you can see the effect of the issue of 10,000 additional ordinary shares at £5 a share and the revaluation of land and buildings, bringing their value up to £200,000.

The value shown for land and buildings has increased by £100,000 because we now believe them to be worth that much more, even though we have not sold any so no cash was received for that increase in valuation.

Cash is up by £50,000, which is the cash we received from the issue of the 10,000 shares at £5 each.

Ordinary shares issued have increased by £10,000, this being the 10,000 shares issued at their £1 nominal value (the value marked on the front of the share certificate).

Capital reserve has increased by £140,000. This was caused by the issue of 10,000 shares at a premium of £4 a share (ie issued at £5 a share with a nominal value of £1 a share) and the revaluation of our land and buildings by an increased £100,000. Our balance sheet now looks like this:

BALANCE SHEET of **AB LTD** as at 30 September 20XX

	£	£
FIXED ASSETS		
Land and buildings	200,000	
Plant and equipment	16,000	
Vehicles	8,000	224,000
INVESTMENTS		
Shares	700	
Equity trusts	4,440	5,140
INTANGIBLE ASSETS		
Goodwill	17,380	
Intellectual property	30,000	47,380
CURRENT ASSETS		
Stock	20,000	
Debtors	1,250	
Cash	51,750	73,000
Total ASSET VALUE		**£349,520**
Less CURRENT LIABILITIES		
Creditors	2,300	
Bank overdraft	5,220	
Taxation	1,250	
Dividends	2,000	10,770
CAPITAL EMPLOYED		**£338,750**
Less LONG-TERM LIABILITIES		
Loans	2,000	
Bonds and Debenture	10,000	
Mortgage	60,000	72,000
Net asset value		**£266,750**
SHAREHOLDERS' FUNDS		
Ordinary shares authorized	50,000	
Ordinary shares issued		30,000
Preference shares		8,000
Capital reserve		190,000
Revenue reserve		38,750
TOTAL SHAREHOLDERS' FUNDS		**£266,750**

Preference shares

Issuing more preference shares is another way the company can raise funds from its shareholders. Preference shares are usually a slightly safer investment for the shareholder than the ordinary shares in that the dividend is often 'guaranteed'. If a company cannot pay the dividends to cumulative preference shareholders (owing to lack of cash or profits) then it must pay them two lots of dividends the following year, before the ordinary shareholders receive anything, and so on.

There are nearly as many variations to the types of preference shares used to raise money as there are to debentures and bonds. The chief difference is that preference shareholders are investors in the company and as such must (like the ordinary shareholders) take their reward via a share of the profits whereas the debenture and bond holders are lenders to the company and so take interest on their money before the profit is calculated.

Revenue reserve

The revenue reserve is the name given to the *retained profits of the company*, ie the profits each year that are not given to the shareholders by way of a dividend. These profits are retained in the business under the assumption that they will help the business grow and become even more profitable.

As we discussed above, the owners of a business (the shareholders) give their money to the company in return for its profits.

When the profit and loss account is completed, everything that is left after all the interest and tax has been paid belongs to the shareholders. (I am not exactly sure that all company directors are fully aware of this fact!)

Shareholders seldom receive the entire profit as a dividend as the directors inevitably recommend that a good proportion be kept by the company for on-going and future investments and expansion. Once the future of the company has been allowed for, the rest is paid to the shareholders by way of a dividend. However, woe betide the chairman who fails to maintain the shareholders' dividend payments.

An interim dividend is normally declared and paid in the latter half of the financial year and a final dividend declared at year-end. As it is shareholders' money that the directors are controlling, the final dividend must be endorsed by the shareholders and this is the subject of a vote at the company's annual general meeting.

Reserves

This is probably the most misleading title of all time. A balance sheet will normally contain the main headings described in this chapter with other details revealed by way of notes attached to the accounts. This saves cluttering up the balance sheet and makes sure that you spend ages digging the relevant information out of the document.

The heading 'reserves' therefore includes the capital and revenue reserve discussed above, and I know of many very senior managers who are happy to see healthy reserves in their company.

In the course of my working life, I have encountered many companies that have needed to find sufficient finance to fund a planned project. In these circumstances, and especially at times when money is particularly tight or interest rates are particularly high, I can guarantee that someone will suggest using the company reserves. After all, they are sitting there waiting to be used, so why don't we finance our next project from them?

At all levels of management there is a common misconception that reserves are great hordes of cash stashed away somewhere for cover in case of bad times, or for some 'rainy-day' investment.

In fact, *reserves contain nothing*.

Reserves merely show where we got the money from in the first place. The money has gone into the cash account and has undoubtedly been spent. There is nothing in reserves!

Many managers find this a very difficult concept to grasp, and it sometimes helps to compare reserves to your own mortgage. At the end of Chapter 1 we listed all you own and all you owed. Among the sums owed was listed mortgage at £60,000.

A mortgage of £60,000 does not mean that you have a reserve of cash amounting to £60,000 that you can use if you need it. It means that you've borrowed £60,000 from a mortgage company and spent it somewhere, presumably on the house.

Inasmuch as there is now no longer any cash to spend, a reserve is similar to a mortgage. It indicates that you have had that value at some time and have used it in the business. It's spent, gone, just like the cash you spent on your mortgage. You may have a house to show for your mortgage and, similarly, you have a business or plant and machinery, or stock or debtors, or whatever you spent it on, to show for the use of the company's reserves.

It is about this stage that managers sometimes get angry and accuse the accountancy profession of completely misleading them. Why call them reserves? Why not call them funds from the shareholders? Or invested profits? Or any other title but one that immediately conjures up pictures of money held in reserve against a downturn or for a rainy day, in the same way as an army has reserves to be called into battle as and when they are needed?

My sympathies are with the non-accountants. Accountants should certainly use terms that everyone understands instead of titles that are almost guaranteed to confuse. There are times when accounting professionals practise their craft in a manner reminiscent of a witch doctor who is afraid that someone else will find the secrets of his potions (and maybe realize how innocuous many really are). Still, I suppose it has its consolations. Have you looked at the accountancy fees in your company lately? We'd never get those levels of fees if we used terms that everyone could understand.

Goodwill

In the last balance sheet you will note that we have an intangible asset called goodwill valued at £17,380. This is the difference between the £80,000 we paid to take your company over, as described at the end of Chapter 1, and the £62,620 worth of net assets we acquired under that transaction. In the UK, goodwill has traditionally been written off against the capital reserve and this has allowed the accountants of past years to considerably distort the comparison of earnings (profits) with the capital employed or the investment made in the company by shareholders.

In the USA, and elsewhere, accountants regard goodwill as an asset that remains with the company for many years ahead (the logic being that if this was not true then you wouldn't have paid the extra £17,380 for it). It doesn't disappear immediately you take over a company.

They therefore treat goodwill in a similar way to their other assets. They enter it on their balance sheet as an asset and then write it off over 40 years in a similar way to depreciation (described above), ie by reducing each year's profits by the amount they have written off the goodwill.

UK accountants used to do something totally different. We wrote it out of our balance sheets immediately by reducing the capital reserve by the amount of goodwill. In fact, we would go further: in assessing goodwill we were allowed to revalue all the assets of the company we had taken over on a 'fair-value' basis.

Fair value is supposed to be the value of an asset, or a liability, as it would be negotiated by two parties on an arm's-length basis. In fact, it was (perhaps still is) often used to provide the value (of the acquisition) that the accountant wanted to see. As a result, in the early 1990s, many companies were hoisted on their own petards of the 'fair values' they had used.

The results of these different treatments can be quite startling, especially in times of high-acquisition activity. The US method reveals higher capital employed and higher shareholders' funds. The UK method dramatically reduces capital employed and shareholders' funds.

US companies must make a return on a higher capital employed than is shown in the books of a UK company, with profits that have been reduced each year by a fortieth of the value of goodwill.

Thankfully, the European Accounting Standards Committee has forced the UK accountants to move towards the US method and write goodwill off over a number of years (they recommend 20). It would certainly be an improvement if both economic and accounting zones agreed to the same number of years – but neither seems to wish to lose their accounting 'virility'.

In the meantime, logic seems to cry out for the value of good-will to be left on the balance sheet. I keep coming back to the fact that the balance sheet should show everything we own and owe at that date.

If the directors of a company have paid far more in a takeover than their target was worth, they should be required to admit to this fact in their report to the shareholders and tell them why they had apparently wasted the shareholders' money. In some instances the increased profitability available from an acquisition justifies paying a premium, but in every case this should be explainable and the accounts should reflect the value of the acquired company at the price paid.

We should show it in the balance sheet at full value and be forced to obtain a return that is commensurate with the money paid for the acquired company.

Our final balance sheet would look like this:

BALANCE SHEET of **AB LTD** as at 30 September 20XX	£	£
FIXED ASSETS		
Land and buildings	200,000	
Plant and equipment	16,000	
Vehicles	8,000	224,000
INVESTMENTS		
Shares	700	
Equity trusts	4,440	5,140
INTANGIBLE ASSETS		
Goodwill	17,380	
Intellectual property	30,000	47,380
CURRENT ASSETS		
Stock	20,000	
Debtors	1,250	
Cash	51,750	73,000
Total ASSET VALUE		**£349,520**
CURRENT LIABILITIES		
Creditors	2,300	
Bank overdraft	5,220	
Taxation	1,250	
Dividends	2,000	10,770
CAPITAL EMPLOYED		**£338,750**
LONG-TERM LIABILITIES		
Loans	2,000	
Bonds and debenture	10,000	
Mortgage	60,000	72,000
Net ASSET VALUE		**£266,750**

SHAREHOLDERS' FUNDS
Ordinary shares	30,000
Preference shares	8,000
Capital reserve	190,000
Revenue reserve	38,750

TOTAL SHAREHOLDERS' FUNDS　　　　**£266,750**

3

What did you earn?

In Chapter 1 we listed everything we own with a monetary value (using no more than common sense to value each item) and called these items assets. We then subtracted everything we owed that has a monetary value (which we called liabilities).

That subtraction left us with a value of our net worth (known to accountants as our net asset value).

We then listed the source from which we originally obtained the cash that made up the net asset value, and if we were a company we agreed that the money probably originated from its owners (the shareholders). The result was our balance sheet.

A balance sheet is merely a simple listing of items that we own and items that we owe, and it can only be correct at one given moment. Tomorrow we will earn some more money, or we will spend some, or incur some debts (such as owe more on our electricity bills, or on our credit cards, etc), and thus our list will change.

If we were a trading company, then each day something would be changing. We would be receiving more stock, making more goods, selling our products, receiving cash from our customers and so on. Our balance sheet can only be completely correct at the moment it is made up and thus its title is always 'as at' a certain date: for example, 'Balance sheet as at 30 September 20XX'.

While the balance sheet gives us a view of our net asset value, it does not tell us how much we are earning.

If you think of the balance sheet as a snapshot of the business, showing all we own and owe at a moment that has been frozen in time, then clearly everything on it is a result of our policies over the period leading up to the date on which we produced it.

We earn over a period of time. We are paid as soon as we have completed a job, or completed a week, a month, a year or some other period of time. Our earnings statement, therefore, cannot be at one precise moment but must cover a given period. Though it could be (and often is) for a week, a month or a quarter, we are going to take a period of one year.

If you were employed then we would start this statement with your annual salary, or the total of 52 weekly pay packets:

<u>Statement of Earnings for One Year
Ending 30 September 20XX</u>

Salary   £25,000

If there were no expenses then that statement on its own would probably be sufficient. However, we want to know how much you earned in that year as a result of selling your services. We know from the above that you earned £25,000, but how much did it cost you to provide that service?

We must deduct all the costs that you incurred over that year, the costs that are directly attributable to you completing that service and earning the £25,000, eg travel (rail fares): £650.

If travel were the only cost that you incurred in that year then your earnings statement would look like this:

<u>Statement of Earnings for Year Ending 30 September 20XX</u>	
Salary	25,000
Less Travel	650
PROFIT	£24,350

We have described the money that you are left with, after deducting the travel costs, as a profit.

It could be that you have spent that 'profit' on other things, such as feeding yourself, paying for clothes, holidays, etc. Profit, therefore, does not indicate that you now still have that amount of cash (£24,350) in the bank, but it does indicate that as a result of selling your services for the year 20XX you were £24,350 better off.

It may be that you incurred other costs in providing that service for the past 12 months, costs that are not so obviously directly linked to the service but without such you could not have provided it. Without getting involved with the UK tax system and whether or not these costs were wholly and exclusively incurred in carrying out your duties, let us assume that you work principally from home and that many of your phone calls are made in pursuance of the service you are providing.

You may also need to use part of your house as an office, completing the paperwork, meeting clients and so on. If so, you incur other costs. We need to deduct these, too, before we know what profit you've really made from providing this service:

<u>Statement of Earnings for Year Ending 30 September 20XX</u>

	£	£
Sale of services		25,000
Less Direct costs		650
GROSS PROFIT		24,350
Less Expenses		
Phone calls	870	
Office costs	380	1,250
TRADING PROFIT		**£23,100**

You will see that we now have two types of profit:

- **Gross profit**, which is the amount we have left from the sales income after deducting all the direct costs.
- **Trading profit**, which is the amount we have left after deducting all the direct costs and the other expenses.

If you were a trading concern then the Inland Revenue would probably now wish to assess you for tax, which is something that we now need to consider:

Statement of Earnings for Year Ending 30 September 20XX		
	£	£
Sale of services	25,000	
Less Direct costs	650	
GROSS PROFIT		**24,350**
Less Expenses		
Phone calls	870	
Office costs	380	1,250
TRADING PROFIT		**£23,100**
Less TAX	3,000	
PROFIT after tax		**£20,100**

You can see that we can define profits at many different levels. The above example shows three levels:

- Gross profit.
- Trading profit.
- Profit after tax.

There are many levels at which profits can be measured. Some are internal, for example factory profits, divisional profits, departmental profits, product profits, etc. Many profit concepts are part of costing systems, but for the moment we will stick to the financial results of your last year's trading and look at those which appear most frequently in a company's annual report and accounts.

Gross profit = sales income less the direct costs of providing the goods or services.

Operating (or *Trading*) *profit* (also known as *PBIT, profit before interest and tax*) = gross profit less all the indirect expenses supporting the provision of the goods or services.

Pre-tax (or *before-tax*) *profits* = operating (trading) profit less any interest incurred on the company's borrowings for the year, plus any interest received.

After-tax profits = pre-tax profits less the tax due as a result of trading for the year.

Retained profits = after-tax profits less any dividend paid or intended to be paid to the shareholders.

To help you to understand the above a little better let us suppose that, instead of being employed with a salary, you and your partner work from home making and selling cuddly toys.

Cuddly toys

You park your cars in front of the house as your garage is given over fully to the making of cuddly toys, and you have a small office over the garage from which you do all the paperwork.

Throughout the last year you have kept a copy of all your sales invoices and all the bills for your expenses. Each quarter you have totalled the VAT on all sales invoices and totalled the VAT on all your purchases. You have then sent the difference to Customs and Excise (the custodians of the VAT collection) in accordance with statutory requirements.

You have written all the details of your sales income and your expenses in a multi-columned book under what you feel are appropriate headings. You have one column for VAT and thus all the rest of the values you enter are the total for goods and services (ie without the VAT included). Your finished list looks a little like this:

SALES	£
Sales invoices for the year	100,000
EXPENSES for the year	£
Purchases of toy-making materials	30,000
Payment to workers making the toys	24,000
Power costs to the garage	2,600
Telephone calls	870
Office costs	3,380
Administration	3,000
Travel and sales promotions	2,700
Delivery of finished goods	1,400
Professional fees	2,600
Interest paid on overdraft	4,000

We can now set these figures out in a way that is both tidier and more useful.

Remember, we are still trying to find out how much you earned last year, but more specifically we want to find out how much you earned from running this small business. We will therefore call the document we are going to produce a profit and loss account.

As it is our first attempt, and we might need further information, we will call it a draft profit and loss account:

CUDDLY TOYS Ltd
DRAFT PROFIT AND LOSS Account
For Year Ending 30 September 20XX

	£	£
Sales		100,000
Less COST OF THE GOODS WE SOLD		
Materials	30,000	
Direct labour	24,000	

Direct expenses	2,600	
Garage wear and tear	3,400	60,000
GROSS PROFIT		40,000
Less OVERHEADS (indirect expenses)		
Telephone costs	870	
Office costs	3,380	
Administration	3,000	
Sales promotions	2,700	
Delivery	1,400	
Professional fees	2,600	
Office equip. depreciation	1,050	15,000
TRADING (operating) profit		25,000
Interest paid	4,000	
PRE-TAX PROFITS		21,000
Taxation	7,000	
AFTER-TAX PROFITS		14,000
Interim dividend (paid)	3,000	
Final dividend (proposed)	5,000	8,000
RETAINED PROFITS for the year		6,000
add Retained profits for		
previous years		68,000
Retained profits c/fwd		£74,000

You will see that all the items from your lists appear in the profit and loss account in what should be a logical sequence. There are a couple of additional items.

We have allowed for the cost of the wear and tear on your garage that has been given over to the business. (If the value of the garage had been included in the balance sheet of Cuddly Toys Ltd as a fixed asset then we would have depreciated that value in the way we described in Chapter 1). In this instance we are assuming that the garage is still really part of the house and we are only charging for the wear and tear caused by running the business from the garage.

Under the heading of overheads, we have depreciated the office equipment by writing the value of the equipment off over its expected lifetime.

From the pre-tax profits, we have calculated the amount we think the tax collector will want from our little company in corporation tax as a result of it making a profit.

We have put all our direct costs and the cost of wear and tear on the garage under the heading *cost of goods sold* (sometimes described as cost of sales).

If we weren't making the cuddly toys ourselves but were buying them in ready made and then selling them on, our only direct costs (and thus the cost of goods sold) would be the cost of the toys. Nearly all the other expenses we incurred would be the costs of supporting the business and would have been shown as overheads. We have chosen to make the toys ourselves, so all the direct costs that are necessary to complete the products get listed before calculating the gross profit.

The type of expenses or costs you would normally see listed under cost of goods sold would be: materials; direct labour; direct expenses; factory costs and so on, ie all the costs of actually making the finished product. The support costs that are necessary to keep the business going are listed under overheads (sometimes called burden, or even simply 'expenses').

The main point to remember here is that, because our document is headed 'the year ending 30 September 20XX', it should only contain sales income and expenditures that are relevant to that year. Anything from another time period would cause major problems.

The sales would be the cash sales plus those sales that were invoiced to customers within that year. (Sale or return invoices would not be included.) Notice it is the invoiced sales, not the cash received from customers, that are shown as sales (or sales turnover).

It may be that you give your customers some period, such as 30 days' credit, in which to pay (which in the UK often means that customers actually take more than 60 days before they send you the money). This does not affect the profit and loss account, which is only interested in the sales you invoiced in the year. (In Chapter 5 we will consider the movement of actual cash through the business, including the cash received from customers as well as the actual invoiced sales within that year.)

This principle of matching sales and expenditure to the period of time covered by the profit and loss account (known by accountants as the accruals principle) applies to all the expenses as well as the sales income. In compiling the profit and loss account we are not so much interested in the actual amount of cash paid out on expenses in the year (that again is the subject of Chapter 5) as we are in the expenses incurred in the year.

Thus, if we paid for some goods in advance then we only include on the profit and loss account the value of the goods we have actually received in the year ending 30 September 20XX. For example, if our £30,000 payment for materials covered the costs of deliveries through this year and some £5,000 for goods that are still to be received after the year-end then we would only include £25,000 as the cost of materials on the profit and loss account.

The payment in advance (£5,000) is, in effect, a debtor (accounts receivable, people who owe us money – see Chapter 1) and, as such, it would be included among the debtors on the balance sheet.

It can be seen, therefore, that the effect of the accruals principle is that the profit and loss account shows the sales and picks up all the expenses that were actually incurred within the period covered by the heading, irrespective of when payment was actually received or made.

If it turned out that only £23,000 worth of materials were needed to satisfy our sales for the year then that is the figure we would enter on our profit and loss account. The remainder (£2,000) would be included as stock (inventory), something to be used during the next year.

The stock left over is deducted from the total cost of purchases for the year and again appears on the balance sheet as something we own, ie it appears on the balance sheet as an asset called stock, listed among the current assets (see Chapter 1).

So, in Cuddly Toys Ltd, of the £30,000 paid out in cash for materials, we now have a figure of £25,000 that appears as purchases. From this we must now deduct £2,000, which represents the stock of material we still had on hand at the close of the year:

Purchases	25,000
less Closing stock	2,000
Cost of materials	£23,000

We must now take care. The material that is in stock at the end of this year will be used during the following 12 months. Therefore, next year's profit and loss will need to reflect the fact that the materials costs contain not only all the purchases that will be received during next year (less any closing stock) but it must also include the value of the stock that it had at the beginning of the year, which has been used to satisfy sales.

The end result of the accruals principle is that materials are calculated as follows:

MATERIALS	£
Opening stock	2,500
plus Purchases for year	25,000
sub-total	27,500
less Closing stock	2,000
Materials used in year	£25,500

A value of £25,500 would therefore be the figure that is used on the profit and loss account to reflect the value of the materials that was contained within the cost of goods sold.

If you grasp the fact that all the accountants are doing with their accruals principle is trying to match income and expenditure to the *period of time*, rather than to movement of cash, then all the above becomes logical.

The accruals principle is fundamental to the way accounts are presented worldwide and it is unfortunate that the simple logic takes a lot of explaining. Once mastered, however, it is easy to apply its logic to every item of income and expenditure.

If your company paid its workers a week late then the accountant, when compiling the profit and loss account, must deduct the first payment of the year from the cash paid for wages (as it related to last year's work). The value of the first payment of the following year would then be added.

In a similar way, if the telephone bill is due at the end of the year, but has not been received, then the accountant must make an accrual, ie use his best judgement as to what the bill should come to, and add that figure to the total value that is shown in the accounts under the heading 'Telephones'.

The adjustments made for accruals have their greatest effect on the figures within the profit and loss account at times when the company is rapidly expanding or contracting, or in times of rapid inflation. For the moment, however, we are going to assume that in Cuddly Toys Ltd all the payments other than materials were for the year, so no other accruals are necessary.

The sales do not need to be adjusted because the figure we have was taken from the invoiced sales. (If we had used the figure shown in the accounts as the amount of cash we received from our customers then it would have needed adjusting by deducting the opening debtors and adding the closing debtors. Opening debtors would be last year's customers who paid us this year; closing debtors would be this year's customers who have not yet paid us.)

Our final profit and loss account, adjusted for accruals and stocks, might look a little like the following:

CUDDLY TOYS LTD
PROFIT AND LOSS Account
For Year Ending 30 September 20XX

	£	£
Sales		100,000
Less COST OF GOODS SOLD		
Materials	25,500	
Direct Labour	24,300	
Direct Expenses	2,600	
Garage Wear and Tear	3,400	55,800
GROSS PROFIT		44,200
Less OVERHEADS (Indirect Expenses)		
Telephone Costs	1,070	

Office Costs	3,380	
Administration	3,000	
Sales Promotions	2,700	
Delivery	1,400	
Professional Fees	2,600	
Office Equip. Depreciation	1,050	15,200
TRADING PROFIT		29,000
Interest paid	4,000	
PRE-TAX PROFITS		25,000
Taxation	8,000	
AFTER-TAX PROFITS		17,000
Interim Dividend (paid)	3,000	
Final Dividend (proposed)	5,000	8,000
RETAINED PROFITS for the year		9,000
add Retained Profits for		
Previous Years		68,000
RETAINED PROFITS c/fwd		£77,000

Remember, all we have done with the above is to take your original list of sales and expenses (as shown on page 55) and adjusted them to reflect the sales and costs that were incurred within the year 20XX, irrespective of when they were received, dispatched or paid for.

It is worth your while taking a moment to compare the above profit and loss account with the list we looked at on page 55. You can see that we have added some depreciation for the garage wear and tear and for the office equipment. The effect of the accruals adjustments are:

● Materials used in the sales for the year are now £25,500.
● Direct labour used in the year is now £24,300.
● Telephones costs for the year are now £1,070.

The effects of the above adjustments are:

- The cost of goods sold (sometimes called the cost of sales) has been reduced to £55,800.
- The gross profit (which is arrived at by deducting the cost of goods sold from the sales) has therefore increased to £44,200.
- The overheads have increased (because of the telephone bill accrual and equipment depreciation) to £15,200.
- Thus the trading profit (sometimes called the operating profit) has increased to £29,000, which after interest gives us pre-tax profits of £25,000.
- Our pre-tax profits are higher. Therefore, we must make a provision for a higher tax charge and this has increased to £8,000, leaving after-tax profits (sometimes called post-tax profits) of £17,000.

We discussed in chapters 1 and 2 the fact that people invest in a company's shares in order to make money. They hope that the company is going to make a profit. It is the profit that is left after all expenses have been paid (and all the interest on the loans and overdrafts has been paid, and after provision has been made for tax) that belongs to the shareholders, ie the after-tax profits.

A company seldom distributes (pays out) all its after-tax profits to its shareholders. It usually retains some of this profit to expand the company, or for other reasons. (As you will see in chapters 5 and 6, it often doesn't have enough cash available to pay it all out even if it wanted to.)

The way profits are paid out to the shareholders is by means of a payment usually made twice a year and known as a *dividend*. An interim dividend is often paid shortly after the six-month results are known, and the directors of a company usually propose a final dividend as part of the annual report and accounts.

The directors must deliver to all shareholders a report of the year's activities and the accounts, ie the balance sheet, the profit and loss account and a *cash flow statement* (sometimes known as the *funds flow*, which we shall be looking at in Chapter 6). The directors must win a vote of approval for the accounts from their shareholders at the annual general meeting (which, I feel, is sometimes given too freely).

The above profit and loss account indicates that the management of Cuddly Toys have earned the shareholders an after-tax profit of £17,000 but, with the anticipated shareholders' approval, they have retained £9,000 to use in the business.

During the year they paid an interim dividend to the shareholders of £3,000 and they have declared a final dividend of £5,000, which will be paid after the AGM (where they are anticipating the shareholders' approval of the accounts). In basic terms, this demonstrates what a profit and loss account is, and why it is produced.

Quite simply, it is the earnings statement of the business. It is sometimes known as the revenue account and is said to contain the running costs of the business.

Expenditure that is included on the profit and loss account is often called the revenue expenditure. (Capital expenditure is the purchase of fixed assets and such expenditures do not appear on the profit and loss account except in the form of one year's depreciation – see Chapter 1.)

When expense is capitalized it means that the costs are deducted from their appropriate headings on the profit and loss account (which are thereby reduced) with the amount of the reduction being shown as a total on the balance sheet as an asset. This will often happen to research and development expense, the writing of computer software, or even the improvement made to land and buildings where a great deal of cost is incurred this year but the benefit is going to be felt over the years ahead.

The profit and loss account should contain the income that has been earned in the year less the expenses of running the business that were incurred in the year and it is sometimes called the company's earnings statement.

So, what do you make of the earnings statement for Cuddly Toys Ltd? How have they done in 20XX?

Is the profit that is revealed a satisfactory result? Has the company made sufficient profit to justify your investment? Should they have paid out more as dividends and retained less to grow the company, or is the reverse true? Do they make sufficient gross profit? Are their overheads too high? Is their stock (inventory) running at the right level? Is it too high? Or too low? Do the accounts provoke any other questions?

Before you reach the end of this book, I hope you will be in a position not only to answer these questions for Cuddly Toys Ltd but also be able to judge for yourself the performance of your own company, division or department – or of any company in which you are interested, or in which you are thinking of investing.

For the moment, let us continue to keep it simple and remember that a balance sheet is a listing of everything that the company owns and everything that it owes, and that the shareholders' funds reveal where the money came from in the first place.

The profit and loss account is the earnings statement of the company and the accountant matches the sales and expenditure to the period of time that is covered by the document. It reveals how much the company has earned over that period.

We shall discover in chapters 5 and 6 that although the company has made a profit, it might have little or no cash. This is not unlike the example at the start of this chapter where you earned a profit of £24,350 from selling your services but would not have that amount now because of all the other things you would need to pay for that were not included in a profit statement.

Chapter 4 takes a detailed look at the profit and loss account and builds upon the knowledge you have gained from this chapter.

To summarize this chapter:

- The balance sheet gives us a view of our net asset value but it does not tell us how much we are earning.
- We earn over a period of time. Therefore, our earnings statement cannot be at one moment in time but must cover a period of an hour, day, week, month, quarter, year, etc.
- There are many levels at which profits can be measured. Some are internal, eg factory profits, divisional profits, departmental profits, product profits, etc.
- Gross profit = sales income less the direct costs of providing the goods or services.
- Operating (or trading) profit (PBIT) = Gross profit less all the indirect expenses supporting the provision of the goods or services.
- Pre-tax (or before-tax) profits = operating (trading) profit less any interest incurred on the company's borrowings for the year, plus any interest received.
- After-tax profits = pre-tax profits less the tax due as a result of trading for the year.

- Retained profits = after-tax profits less any dividend paid or intended to be paid to the shareholders.
- The type of expenses or costs you would normally see listed under cost of goods sold (sometimes called cost of sales) would be: materials, direct labour, direct expenses, factory costs and so on, ie all the costs of actually making the finished product.
- The support costs that are necessary to keep the business going are listed under overheads
- The sales would be the cash sales plus those sales that were invoiced to customers within that year. (Sale or return invoices would not be included.) NB it is the invoiced sales and not the cash received from customers that is shown as sales (or sales turnover).
- It may be that you give your customers some period, such as 30 days' credit, in which to pay. This does not affect the profit and loss account, which is only interested in the sales you invoiced in the year.
- This principle of matching sales and expenditure to the period of time covered by the profit and loss account (known by accountants as the accruals principle) applies to all the expenses as well as the sales income.
- In compiling the profit and loss account we are not so much interested in the actual amount of cash paid out on expenses in the year (that again is the subject of Chapter 5) as we are in the expenses incurred in the year.
- It can be seen that the effect of the accruals principle is that the profit and loss account shows the sales and picks up all the expenses that were actually incurred within the period covered by the heading, irrespective of when payment was actually received or made.
- The stock (inventory) left over is deducted from the total cost of purchases for the year and appears on the balance sheet as something we own, ie it appears on the balance sheet as an asset called stock, listed among the current assets (see Chapter 1).
- The material that is in stock at the end of this year will be used during the following 12 months. Therefore, next year's profit and loss will need to reflect the fact that the materials costs contain not only all the purchases that will be received during next year (less any closing stock) but it must also include the

value of the stock that it had at the beginning of the year, which has been used to satisfy sales.

● If you grasp the fact that all the accountants are doing with their accruals principle is trying to match income and expenditure to the *period of time*, rather than to movement of cash, then all the above becomes logical.

● The accruals principle is fundamental to the way accounts are presented worldwide and it is unfortunate that the simple logic takes a lot of explaining. Once mastered, however, it is easy to apply its logic to every item of income and expenditure.

● It is the profit that is left after all expenses have been paid (and all the interest on the loans and overdrafts has been paid, and after provision has been made for tax) that belongs to the shareholders, ie the after-tax profits.

● A company seldom distributes (pays out) all its after-tax profits to its shareholders. It usually retains some of this profit to expand the company.

● The way profits are paid out to the shareholders is by means of a payment usually made twice a year and known as a dividend.

● An interim dividend is often paid shortly after the six-month results are known, and the directors of a company usually propose a final dividend as part of the annual report and accounts.

● The directors must deliver to all shareholders a report of the year's activities and the accounts, ie the balance sheet, the profit and loss account and a cash flow statement sometimes known as the funds flow.

● The profit and loss account is the earnings statement of the business.

● The profit and loss account is sometimes known as the revenue account and it is said to contain the running costs of the business.

● Expenditure that is included on the profit and loss account is often called revenue expenditure. (Capital expenditure is the purchase of fixed assets and such expenditures do not appear on the profit and loss account except in the form of one year's depreciation).

● When expense is capitalized it means that the costs are deducted from their appropriate headings on the profit and loss account (which are thereby reduced) with the amount of the reduction being shown as a total on the balance sheet as an asset. This will often happen to research and development expense, the writing of computer software, or even the improvement made to land and buildings.

- The profit and loss account should contain the income that has been earned in the year less the expenses of running the business that were incurred in the year, and it is sometimes called the company's earnings statement.

- Continue to keep it simple and remember that a balance sheet is a listing of everything that the company owns and everything that it owes, and the shareholders' funds reveal where the money came from in the first place.

- The profit and loss account is the earnings statement of the company and the accountant matches the sales and expenditure to the period of time that is covered by the document. It reveals how much the company has earned over that period.

4

The profit and loss account

Chapter 3 described the profit and loss account – the company's statement of earnings – and the accruals principle. If you missed that chapter for any reason then it is worth spending a moment or two reviewing the bullet-point summary in its last few pages before commencing Chapter 4.

In this chapter, we will examine the profit and loss account line by line. Later, we will consider that buzzword of so many managements at the end of the twentieth century – the bottom line!

'We're bottom-line managers.' 'We're a bottom-line company.' 'In our company, we manage by the bottom line.' These or similar phrases were, and still are, often heard from managers attending seminars and workshops.

During the course of this chapter, and the rest of the book, we will see how many of these 'bottom-line' managers opt out of their financial responsibility by implementing little more than a buzzword. It is no coincidence that many companies managed in this way suffered acute financial problems, or even collapsed in liquidation, during the recession of the early 1990s. I'm sure that many more will follow suit in the great recession due in 2010 and 2031.

For the moment, we will look at a profit and loss account for AB Ltd for the year ending 31 December 20XX:

AB LTD
PROFIT AND LOSS Account
For Year Ending 31 December 20XX

	£	£
SALES		1,000,000
Less COST OF GOODS SOLD		
Materials	190,000	
Direct labour	290,000	
Factory expenses	95,000	575,000
GROSS PROFIT		425,000
Less OVERHEADS (indirect expenses)		
Administration	130,000	
Sales and Advertising	170,000	
Delivery	45,000	
Professional Fees	15,000	360,000
TRADING PROFIT		65,000
Interest paid		12,000
PRE-TAX PROFITS		53,000
Taxation		16,000
AFTER-TAX PROFITS		37,000
Interim Dividend (paid)	10,000	
Final Dividend (proposed)	15,000	25,000
RETAINED PROFITS for the year		12,000
add Retained Profits for Previous Years		26,750
TOTAL RETAINED PROFITS c/fwd		£38,750

The title

You will notice that whereas the balance sheet can only be documented as at one moment, providing a snapshot of all that the company owned and owed at that time, the profit and loss account must be for a period of time. It can be for any period but the most common are weekly, monthly, quarterly, half-yearly and annually.

The published financial accounts of a company are normally produced annually with an abbreviated set of accounts produced at the half-year. In this chapter we are considering the profit and loss for the year.

If the company is a trading company then it will normally attempt to sell its goods and services for more than it costs to produce them in order to produce a profit for its owners (the shareholders).

If it is not a trading company, or is a non-profit-making organization, company or trust, then it will try to make sure that it has more income than expenditure (or at least not have more expenditure than income). Almost the same rules apply except that the document is called an income and expenditure account instead of a profit and loss account.

Instead of sales, the non-profit company would start its document with income and detail the main sources. It would then deduct expenditure to give a surplus of income over expenditure, or an excess of expenditure over income.

A trading company starts the profit and loss account with sales (sometimes called turnover or revenue). Sales should be the invoiced sales for the year covered by the profit and loss account (excluding any VAT or sales tax) plus any cash sales – it is not calculated solely on the cash received from customers.

The cash received by the company from its customers within that year must be adjusted by deducting any VAT or sales tax that is collected on behalf of the government (and has no benefit to the company save the cash holding before it is remitted).

You must also adjust for any discounts your customers may have taken as these are usually treated as an expense on the profit and loss account. The sales are grossed up by adding back the discounts and then the discounts are deducted as an expense.

From the total cash received in the year, you must deduct the value of the opening debtors and then add on the value of the goods provided to your closing debtors. Opening debtors are last year's customers who paid us this year; closing debtors are this year's customers who have not yet paid us. The reason for these adjustments is the accruals principle, which matches all actions to the period of time rather than to the cash received or paid.

Although we often describe sales as the invoiced sales for the year, it would be more correct to think of them as the sales for which the company's customers are legally bound to pay. In AB Ltd our sales for the year after all these adjustments were £1,000,000.

Any goods or services that were provided on a sale-or-return basis should not be included in the figure until the return part of the agreement no longer applies. Similarly, invoices that have been sent out where no work has been undertaken, nor goods dispatched to the customer (or invoices for goods that are not according to contract), should not be included.

I am sometimes asked to explain this last statement by managers who assure me that such actions are standard practice in their companies at period-ends and year-ends. I am told that it is done with the full knowledge of the senior management and the intention is solely to push sales up for that particular period.

The only comment that can be made is that such actions are questionable and I feel sure that they must be mistaken, or at least their accountants know nothing of this practice. Our task as accountants is to produce accounts that show a true and fair view of the activities of the company over the stated period of time. Remember, if you sail too close to the wind, you are in grave danger of capsizing.

The more the figures are 'adjusted' (and it is common practice in so many companies and organizations), the more they become the shifting sands on which management tries to base decisions, with the inevitable results.

The cost of goods sold

The cost of goods sold (sometimes called the cost of sales) collects all the 'direct costs' of the company, ie the costs that are directly associated with the products or services the company provides to its customers. The direct costs are the materials that go into the product, and the people who work on it as it passes through the factory, as well as the factory costs themselves.

In a service industry, the cost of sales would include the cost of the people working directly on the customers' contracts, ie the specialists dedicated to the customers' work. The cost of providing that service would include the cost of their travel to and from the customers' premises, their subsistence and accommodation (which the company pays on their behalf).

In the case of service and manufacturing industries, the attempt is much the same. We wish to identify a gross profit, ie how much we have left from sales after providing the service, or producing the goods. The gross profit must be enough to pay our support operations, as well as the interest on our borrowings and tax, and still leave enough to reward our shareholders adequately for giving us the money to manage the company.

Gross profit is arrived at from sales less cost of goods sold (or cost of sales). Let us look in more detail at the costs (which should be exclusive of VAT in companies registered for this tax) that make up the cost of goods sold.

The types of heading usually found in the cost of goods sold are: materials; direct labour; factory costs.

Materials

When 'materials' is used as a heading to indicate the amount of purchases that have been used in production then it includes the cost of: raw materials; plus the value of work-in-progress; plus the value of finished goods.

It is often difficult to identify the actual items of material that were included in the products sold, so the cost of materials is usually calculated in the following way:

First, we take the stock (inventory) that was on hand at the end of previous year. For example: opening stock: £22,000. Second, we add the purchases of materials we have made throughout the year: purchases: £188,000. The resultant sum of £210,000 is, theoretically, the amount of materials we have available to be sold (£22,000 + £188,000).

If we now deduct the value of the stock we have left at the end of the year then we can assume that the difference is the value of the materials that went out of the company in sales during the year. Taking the value of the closing stock to be £20,000, the value of the materials to be included in the cost of goods sold in the year would be calculated thus:

Opening stock	22,000
(plus) Purchases	<u>188,000</u>
(thus) Available for sale	210,000
(less) Closing stock	<u>20,000</u>
Materials in cost of sales	£190,000

Direct labour

Direct labour includes the cost of the workers who actually turn the products and services into something that can be sold to the company's customers. Supervisors and managers are usually listed amongst the overheads under an appropriate heading, eg production or management.

If there are wages and other direct labour costs for the year then they are included in this figure. If they work a week in advance then the first payment of the year belongs to the preceding year's profit and loss account, whereas the first payment next year belongs to this year's profit and loss account (accruals principle, see previous chapter).

The cost of direct labour to AB Ltd in the year was £290,000.

Factory expenses

Factory expenses usually include all the costs associated with the actual place where the work is done (ie the factory as opposed to the offices). They normally include any premises costs such as rent or repairs to the factory, as well as depreciation (see Chapter 2) on the factory buildings and on the plant and machinery used in the factory.

The cost of factory expenses to AB Ltd in the year was £95,000.

At this stage, many textbooks start looking at the alternatives to the cost of goods sold and give graphic descriptions of manufacturing accounts and trading accounts and get very excited about prime costs, costs of production and so on.

They are correct to do so as most academic examinations still include such items. The purpose of this book, however, is to give the reader as much practical knowledge as possible, and *How to Master Finance* therefore concentrates on the practical. In all the years I have been in senior line-management, and in consultancy, in both manufacturing and service industries, I have never come across the use of manufacturing accounts or prime costs in practice. A word with many of my financial colleagues reveals much the same story. Undoubtedly such accounts must exist, but they are such a rarity in real life that I have left their descriptions to the academics. Those who need to know about them can find descriptions in most good textbooks on bookkeeping and accounts.

Gross profit

Is this the bottom line?

Gross profit is calculated by deducting the cost of goods sold (cost of sales) in the period covered by the profit and loss account from the sales of that same period.

Gross profit, when expressed as a percentage of sales, can be a key management ratio and of tremendous help, along with other key ratios, in managing a company, or even part of a company (see Chapter 9).

Unfortunately it is often impossible to calculate the gross profit of companies from their published accounts as the cost of goods sold is often not revealed. (It is, therefore, often missing from databases that contain company results.) It is, however, sometimes possible to look at the company's annual report and accounts and work out the gross profit from the notes that are attached to the profit and loss account. It is usually readily available within the company from its management reports.

It is at the gross profit stage of the profit and loss account that the maximum profit is usually found. Remember that at this stage we have turned the goods or services into a saleable condition and have deducted the costs of so doing from the invoiced sales of the period.

The next stage on the profit and loss account is to deduct all the remaining running costs of the company. In other words, we are now going to use up some of the profit we have generated.

It is at this next stage that so many companies lose their way and so many managers lose sight of the company's main purpose – to make money for its owners.

We know that the avowed purpose of nearly every person who holds shares (or is in a company's share option scheme) is to make money. The shareholders delegate to the management of a company the task of maximizing profits, and most shareholders are happy to reward the management and workforce for so doing. *The gross profit is, however, the point at which that purpose is fulfilled.* From that point on, the company is spending its profits, ie spending its shareholders' money.

It is my contention that a management team's first priority should be to maximize gross profit, and that the only reason for expenditure from that point onwards is to increase (or at worse maintain) that gross profit. Experience reveals that this is far from the case in many companies and that the larger a company becomes, the more it loses sight of those priorities.

Whole departments have come into being to do very little else but produce memos and reports (thus stopping everyone who is required to read them from doing something practical and improving the profits). Just how much of the paper or data that is shifted around companies in this information age has any impact on actually improving profits is debatable. I suspect very little.

One of the classic symptoms of this problem is often the monthly management report. Accountants and computer systems managers produce management reports with great pride (and often at great costs in equipment and expensive people). It is not unusual for the reports to be 20 or more pages long and packed with 'vital' information to be read and digested each month. The problem is that so few of these specialists have taken the trouble to find out what the recipients of the reports do with them. Do they look at them? If so what do they look at, and act upon, to improve the profit of the company?

Many output audits on modern management reports reveal that most contain far too much information for the time that is available to the recipient to study them. Most are too complex for the user who, at best, will look at only half a dozen figures. Some people never look at them at all! They take them to read at home and then bring them back the next day unread, and will often repeat this action on every day of the month until next month's arrives; then the old one gets assigned to the waste-paper bin and the process starts all over again.

If the above is true (and it is extremely close to the truth in an awful lot of cases), then why are we wasting the shareholders' money in producing this expensive document in the first place? Why not produce a report that contains just the half-dozen figures that the user will act upon to improve or maintain profits, and thus save the considerable cost of the people, equipment, paper, and time, that is involved in the present systems?

It is not only accountants that are beavering away to complete a task that has little or no effect on profits. The bigger the company, the more individuals get involved in tasks that make little or no difference to profits; indeed, the purpose of whole departments becomes the completion of a daily task rather than the selling of goods and services for more than it costs to produce them.

How often do you hear staff curse the fact that the customers keep on getting in the way of completing the important task they are trying to do? Stand in a bank and count how many people there are working away at the back compared to the one or two who are attempting to cope with the growing queue of customers (and one of those will inevitably be locked into some lengthy query).

Does it happen in your company? Only you can answer that question but, in the meantime, the foregoing should have focused your mind sharply on the overheads that the company has (and why they exist?). US accountants often use the title of burden to describe overheads, and it may well be a better, or more apt, title.

It is little wonder that the 'downsizers' had such easy targets in the 1990s for the overhead and management structure of so many businesses dated back to the pre-computer days. Despite all the electronic assistance now available to businesses and organizations one thing is guaranteed – overheads will continue to grow in most companies throughout the twenty-first century, and the downsizers will continue to make a pretty penny for some time to come.

Overheads

Overheads contain all the costs that the company has incurred (with the exception of interest received and paid) other than the direct costs that were included in the cost of goods sold (the cost of sales).

There are no firm headings for this section and the actual headings and amount of detail will vary considerably between the management accounts (where the maximum number of headings is often used) and the published financial accounts (where it is often necessary to look at the notes to discover more than one heading).

Some examples of overheads are: administration, sales and advertising, delivery and professional fees. You should remember that this is the section that also picks up the depreciation (see Chapter 1) of non-production buildings, equipment and vehicles.

The depreciation is usually included in the appropriate costs (eg administration includes one year's depreciation of the office equipment and furniture). The management accounts will break these costs down in detail by department or company.

We look a little closer at overheads, and their control, in Chapter 9. In the meantime, we need to keep in mind that the overheads are deducted from the gross profit to give the trading profit.

For example:

GROSS PROFIT		£425,000
Less OVERHEADS (indirect expenses)		
Administration	130,000	
Sales and Advertising	170,000	
Delivery	45,000	
Professional Fees	15,000	360,000
TRADING PROFIT		£65,000

Trading profit

Is *this* the bottom line?

The trading (sometimes called operating) profit should be of critical interest to all managers. It is the measure of their performance.

The shareholders have delegated the management of the company to its directors and managers, and it is the trading profit that provides a measure of how well they have managed the amount of capital that is employed in the company.

When we were looking at the balance sheet in chapters 1 and 2, we agreed that the capital employed was a measure of the funds that were available to the managers of a company. Capital employed could be arrived at by taking the total assets and deducting the current liabilities, but it also equates to the sum of the shareholders' funds and the long-term liabilities (ie the funds locked into the company for its management to use).

We discussed what sort of return we, as shareholders, should get for our money and agreed that it should at least be more than we could get if we put the equivalent amount of money into a safe haven like a bank or a building society. In the 1990s this gave us a required return on the capital employed in the company in excess of 16 per cent, but 12 per cent or more might satisfy a shareholder in the days of low interest.

We also realized that, as the capital employed was the total of shareholders' funding plus long-term liabilities, we needed to earn a higher return on the money we have borrowed than the actual cost of borrowing. If we failed to achieve this then it would be better not to borrow in the first place: we'd be better off financially, less at risk – and more profitable.

Furthermore, if the company had a significant overdraft then it needed to earn even more on the borrowed money. Otherwise the company is not only working for the banks instead of its shareholders, but it is also gradually using up all its cash and profits in meeting the bank interest payments.

The measure of the return on the capital employed in the company is the trading (operating) profit. The trading profit, when expressed as a percentage of the capital employed, needs to be significantly (traditionally 8–10 per cent) above the cost of borrowing (otherwise don't risk the shareholders' funds).

The trading profit is, therefore, of critical interest to every manager and it is not just the absolute figure but its relationship to the amount of capital employed that is important.

There may be very legitimate reasons for effectively reducing the capital employed (as shown on the balance sheet) by writing out the goodwill, or failing to revalue assets where they are significantly undervalued, or removing properties off the balance sheet completely, but I think few of these moves can be justified. The true purpose of many companies employing these tactics is probably to keep down the value of the capital employed and thus make the management performance appear much better than it really is. With such tactics employed to depress the values shown on the balance sheet, it is little wonder that there are such rich pickings for the predatory asset-stripping company.

Maximizing the trading profit (ie 'we concentrate on the

bottom line') without taking account of the capital employed (calculated on a 'true and fair view' basis) is a recipe that often leads to disaster.

We need to make enough trading profit to be able to pay all the interest incurred in the year, and to cover the amount necessary to pay tax. Once we have covered those, the rest is left for the shareholders, as we can see from the following example:

Trading profit	£65,000
Interest	12,000
Pre-tax profits	53,000
Taxation	16,000
After-tax profits	£37,000

Interest

Interest is the amount of interest incurred on all loans and borrowings (including bank overdraft) over the period of time that is covered by the profit and loss account, less the interest received on any funds that may have qualified for interest.

Some companies may have earned more interest on deposits than they paid on loans. Although this may seem at first sight to be good management, the shareholders are usually unimpressed.

They have invested in the company to obtain a return on capital employed in excess of the return that they can get from putting their money in interest-bearing investments. They could put their money into a bank or building society, or on the overnight market. They want their money in the company to earn about 8–10 per cent more than is otherwise obtainable. That's why they invested it in the business in the first place.

If the management cannot use the shareholders' cash to produce the required profits then it should, logically, return their money (via a dividend payment or share buy-back scheme) and allow the shareholders to invest it themselves.

It is for this reason that shareholders do not approve of a company sitting on high cash holdings, but be aware that a high cash holding in a company can often signify that it will be acting in the predator role in some takeover activity in the near future.

Pre-tax profits

Is *this* the bottom line?

Some companies hold their management responsible for all their borrowings and thus place great emphasis on the pre-tax profits. They assume the same importance as the trading profit and sufficient return must be made on the investment that is represented by the capital employed.

Other companies concentrate their efforts on continually improving the pre-tax profits as the lowest point on the profit and loss account at which management control exists. The thinking is often that tax is governed by the rules of the capital allowances that are included in each year's Finance Act. The Finance Act defines the details of the capital allowances that a company may claim and thus tax is, to a certain extent, outside the control of the management of a company. However, a good tax accountant can be worth his or her weight in profit in allowing the company to make the best 'use' of the tax laws.

Maximizing pre-tax profits (ie 'we're a bottom-line company') without taking account of the capital employed (calculated on a 'true and fair view' basis) is another recipe that often leads to disaster.

Taxation

Many European countries have much firmer rules of accounting than the UK, and in many of these countries the government sets the amount of depreciation that can be allowed against fixed assets. It then becomes allowable as an expense on the profit and loss account, so reducing the profit on which tax must be paid.

In the UK, you can choose your own method of depreciation, and the length of time over which you are going to depreciate the asset. The only real constraint is that if a company alters the basis of its depreciation charges then the accountant should carry a note on the annual accounts revealing the effect this change has had on profits. The Inland Revenue does not allow depreciation as an allowable expense even though it has been included as an expense item in the profit and loss account.

If the tax collector is happy with the way the pre-tax profits have been accounted for, he or she will then add back the amount that was deducted from profits as an expense under the heading of depreciation, and thus increase the pre-tax profits by that amount. He or she then deducts the capital allowances that are allowable to the company under the current Finance Act to arrive at a taxable profit. Tax is then calculated on that taxable profit at the rate of corporation tax that the government has decreed as payable.

Let's look at an example:

PRE-TAX PROFITS		£53,000
add back Depreciation		5,000
Adjusted PROFIT		58,000
Less CAPITAL ALLOWANCES		
First Year Allowance	6,000	
Writing-down Allowance	4,000	10,000
TAXABLE PROFITS		£48,000
Taxation @ 33%	£16,000	

Capital allowances

These are totally dependent upon the government (and their need to collect taxes).

In the past few decades we have seen the tax rate for corporation tax vary from 52 per cent of the taxable profits down to 25 per cent. During the same period, the first-year allowances have ranged from 100 per cent of the value of the plant and equipment that the company purchased in that year, through 75 per cent, then 50 per cent to end the millennium at 25 per cent.

Thus, at the start of the decade, the full value of any new or reconditioned capital plant or equipment (ie new fixed assets) was deducted from the adjusted profits to give the taxable profit. By the 1990s that allowance had fallen to 25 per cent of the value.

All was not lost, however, as the 75 per cent not allowed in the first year did fall to the writing-down allowance. This lets the company claim 25 per cent of the written-down value each following year. If the asset is eventually sold then a balancing charge or balancing allowance comes into being.

The UK does have rules governing tax allowances for depreciation that are broadly similar to European rules, but they are made a separate calculation from the figures that are shown on the published accounts.

Why this should be, and what the advantages are, I once again leave to the academic accountants.

After-tax profits

Is *this* the bottom line?

Well, yes, it is, but it isn't the one that most managers are talking about when they describe themselves as 'bottom-line managers'.

Most managers refer to the bottom line on their management report, or the company's profit. But to which profit are they referring when they speak of the 'bottom line'? Is it the gross profit or the trading profit? Is it the pre-tax profit, the after-tax profit or the retained profits?

The answers I have received to these questions leaves me convinced that 'bottom-line management' was, and is, merely a buzzword used to cover up the evasion of financial responsibility.

What is more, bottom-line management is normally accompanied by a complete lack of management of anything but the profit figure that makes up this mysterious 'bottom line'. Over the last two decades, managers proudly boasting that they were excellent 'bottom-line' managers were making decisions that undoubtedly increased profits, but also sent their companies spiralling down towards liquidation.

The lesson is that you cannot manage on bottom line alone. There is more to a business than profit. There is the cost of the investment that is made to increase that profit, the true cost of money paid out for acquisitions (not the fair-value adjustments that are written off against the reserves) and the satisfactory return to the owners (the shareholders).

Even more important than managing the profit and loss and the balance sheet is the vital task of managing cash – the lifeblood of the company.

Cash management must be of vital concern to every manager in the company. Without it, the manager has no company, and hence no job.

The fact that so many managers have given the company's cash resources so little thought over the years is a great credit to the abilities of their accountants.

In many companies it is assumed that the accountant will have the money available to meet all the company plans and to cover the day-to-day expenditure. Most of them do, and at the treasury function they have few equals. There is, however, much more to cash management than the treasury function alone, and no manager is worthy of that title until he or she fully understands, and uses, sensible and wise cash management.

We look at cash management in chapters 5 and 6. In the meantime, we have profits (but maybe no cash) available for the shareholders. We have after-tax profits. This is the value that is left for the shareholders after all the direct costs have been paid, all the expenses have been paid, and the interest and tax have been allowed for. It is the pursuit of after-tax profits that caused the Shareholders to invest in the company. Do they get it all? Probably not.

The board of directors decide, first, how much they can afford to pay as a dividend (there may be no cash in the company) and, second, how much they wish to retain within the company to pay for future expansion.

Remember, if they are retaining shareholders' cash then the managers of the company are making an implied promise that they will continue to give the same level of return on the retained cash as the shareholders are enjoying on their present investment. Profits must therefore increase yet further next year to cover the return on the retained profits.

Finally, the directors decide how much they can give their shareholders now by way of dividend to keep them happy, and then the whole proposal goes to the annual general meeting for the shareholders' approval.

So, having got after-tax profits, we deduct the dividend we are paying to the shareholders to reveal the amount of retained profits for the year. We add the retained profits from all the preceding years the company has been trading to get the total retained profits. Our profit and loss account is complete:

AFTER-TAX PROFITS		£37,000
Interim Dividend (paid)	10,000	
Final Dividend (proposed)	15,000	25,000
RETAINED PROFITS for the year		12,000
add Retained Profits for		
Previous Years		26,750
Total RETAINED PROFITS c/fwd		38,750

It is the total retained profits that appears as the revenue reserve, which is shown as part of the shareholders' funds on the balance sheet.

Many people have difficulty in seeing why the £12,000 retained profits for the year, and the £26,750 from previous years, isn't a pool of cash that they can use for whatever they want in the business. The answer to this is similar to the situation that confronted you at the start of Chapter 3 when you earned a profit of £24,350 from selling your services. However, that money had also paid for your personal food costs, for finance payments you were making on your car, for your holiday and the repayment of the bank loan. At no time during the year did you have that amount of money in your personal bank account. Indeed, your bank statement could well have been printed in red ink. You were earning the money each week throughout the year but you were also spending it on items not included in your earnings statement.

So it is with a company. A company spends its cash throughout the year on many things that do not appear on the profit and loss account. For example, capital expenditure (cash spent on purchasing new fixed assets). The entire cost of the new fixed asset may be paid for out of cash but only the depreciation for the period will be shown on the profit and loss account.

The profit and loss account does not include the cost of any acquisitions your company may have made in the past year.

The profit and loss account does not include the cost of repayments of loans. It includes the interest paid on loans, but not the repayments of the borrowed sum.

The profit and loss account does not include as a cost any

increase in stock (inventory) values, or the amount of money owed to you by your debtors (customers) – and so on.

The money that you have been generating through the year's trading, as represented on your profit and loss account, could well have been used for many, if not all, of these various cases.

Indeed, it may have been necessary to raise further funds to pay for them all, funds that again do not get included on the profit and loss account as they did not come about by trading or operating profitably. Examples would include:

- Funds raised from a new issue of shares.
- Raising new loans.
- Selling existing fixed assets.
- Reducing stocks or debtors.
- Increasing creditors (ie time taken to pay suppliers).

Even before you get to the end of the year, the profit that you have worked so hard to make could all be gone, and you might be facing tough times ahead. If you are really unlucky you might even be staring at the liquidator.

The profit and loss account is a vital document and it is delegated to the manager to produce sufficient trading profit to give the required return on capital employed (ROCE). You also need to ensure that the shareholders' after-tax profits give them the earnings they require from the company (ROI – return on investment).

The profit and loss, however, is not a document that is to be managed to the exclusion of all others (as in 'bottom-line' companies). It has its place, and it is important, but it is hoped that by the time you have completed this book you will be managing the profit, the cash and the balance sheet with equal vigour.

Profits are vital – they are to the corporate body what food is to the human body. Without them we starve, eventually to death; although we can linger for many days without food, we are getting ever weaker.

Cash is the lifeblood of the corporate body and just as the human being will rapidly expire if the bleeding is not stopped, so will the corporate body.

5

Cut your coat according to your cloth!

If you have read the earlier chapters then you will have realized that an abundance of common sense and a modicum of enthusiasm (or the other way about) are really all you need to understand balance sheets and profit and loss accounts. Exactly the same goes for cash management, whether in the home or in business.

In the same way as any family in the western world needs cash to pay for all its needs, so does a business. If you run out of cash you can go to your bank manager to try to borrow some by taking out a loan or an overdraft, and so can a business. If you completely run out of cash then you just have to do without until you have earned some more or raised some more, and so it is with a business.

Cash is as vital to a business as any other resource. In fact, cash is the most vital resource of all. Without cash the business cannot pay its workers their wages, it cannot pay its suppliers, or interest on its loans, or the Inland Revenue its dues. It is a situation that rapidly deteriorates into disaster and bankruptcy.

The same is true at home. If you fail to pay your mortgage then eventually the building society will come along and seize your house, ousting you into the street. If you fail to pay your rent then a similar fate awaits you. If you fail to repay the instalments on a purchase you made under a credit agreement then you will get chased through the courts for payment and, in certain circumstances, you may finish up by losing the thing that you purchased as well as paying out a great deal of money for the privilege.

In view of the undoubted importance of managing our cash, it seems strange how little education is given to this aspect of life. Cash management is so rarely taught, even in management colleges, despite the fact that it is going to be of vital importance to nearly everybody for the rest of their lives.

One of the strange things about cash is the way we 'live up to it'. Most people manage to pay their way week by week, month by month, in many cases leaving little if any surplus over at month-end. If we suddenly get a rise in income, maybe a significant rise well above the level of inflation, within months we are still only just managing to pay our way with little or no surplus.

Money is effectively a resource, rather like time. There is, in fact, plenty of it for most people in the western world – enough to do all we could reasonably want, if only we could organize ourselves to manage it properly. Sadly, it is this that is the undoing of so many of us. We fail to organize and manage the resources of cash and time, and so they seem to run out with increasing rapidity.

It is not usually the level of income that is the problem but the way we manage it (or rather the way we fail to manage it). Cash must be separated from profits or any other accounting expression. Profit is the difference in value between the net worth (net asset value) of yourself, or of a company, at the beginning of the year and at the end of that year.

Cash is the actual money that you have at any one moment, either in your pocket or purse, or in your bank account. *Cash management* is the skill of ensuring that there is always enough cash available to meet the requirement of yourself or your company. Cash management is also the skill of managing the needs of yourself or your company to match the cash resources that can be made available.

It is in this area that so many accountants are outstanding. They manage to keep many companies afloat and paying their way despite the avoidance of cash responsibility by many non-financial managers. Indeed, the action of many non-financial managers is directly contrary to the requirements of sound cash management.

One of the principal reasons for this disturbing fact is the result of the manager believing that his or her function, such as selling, production or administration, can be undertaken in isolation, with no consideration given to the effect of their actions on the vital cash resource of the business.

Thankfully, the days of this kind of managerial ignorance are diminishing as more and more management education takes place. It is unfortunate, however, that on many management courses a great deal of emphasis is placed on esoteric subjects such as mission statements, strategic thinking, assertive training, employee sensitivities and so on. These subjects do, indeed, have merit, but perhaps they should not be given pride of place before the manager has mastered the financial facts of life, or at least been given the opportunity to focus on what he or she is employed to do, ie maximize the return to the shareholders.

(If you don't believe that maximizing the return to the share-holders is the primary function of a business ask any shareholder why they hold their shares in a company and how long they would keep them if their returns failed to keep pace with infla-tion year in, year out.)

Good strategy is undoubtedly vital to a business, but the best strategy in the world will not replace a lack of cash, or the lack of ability to pay our bills. (Just try paying a supplier with your strategy document or your mission statement.)

We really must get the fundamentals of cash management and profit maximization well into the subconscious of every one of our managers before we embark upon more grandiose thoughts.

Much of my consultancy work is concerned with refocusing managers at all levels of a company's hierarchy to their responsi-bilities for the financial health of the company. By introducing them to sound techniques and principles we help clients to achieve outstanding results, often in the most difficult economic or trading circumstances.

Directors of companies are often startled by how much money can be extracted from the idle or under-utilized assets of their seemingly well-managed companies. The cash generated can either be used to pay off the highest-interest loans or ploughed back into the profitable parts of the business thus enhancing profits at no cost to the investors.

On many occasions, companies try the in-house approach but achieve only limited success. The reason for our success, as consultants, is the fact that we are not subject to the cultural barriers that have been set up within each organization, either consciously or unconsciously. We are not affected by the 'tribal' behaviours within functional management that often make it almost impossible to achieve success from within the company itself.

The greatest problem to be faced is that most non-financial managers take little or no responsibility for the cash management of the business and just do not understand it. They might give lip-service to the accountant at meetings and nod in what they hope is the correct manner when vital areas of financial management are discussed but deep down many are frightened by their lack of financial knowledge.

The key to success is first to refocus managers to the fundamental importance of cash management, and then to point them in the direction of sound cash management within their own organization.

The returns on such a task can be enormous, far beyond the costs. Hopefully this book will help to provide you with the tools to manage this task for yourselves, or at least to understand the techniques that prove to be successful all over the world.

The fundamental message that every manager must appreciate is that cash management is the number one responsibility of everyone in the business. Without it, there is no business.

For the moment let us think about managing ourselves. Let us look at our own cash management. In Chapter 1 we looked at our own list of all we owned and all we owed, and we formed it into a balance sheet. In Chapter 3 we looked at our income statement and put together our profit and loss account. Let us now progress from those financial statements and look at our cash flow.

You will remember from the profit and loss account that we showed an income of £25,000 from selling our services. Suppose that income is the result of a substantial rise in the year to 30 September 20XX, and we decide to celebrate our good fortune by splashing out on a good holiday. We also need a car and a new dining-room suite. Our personal profit and loss account (Chapter 3, page 53) shows an after-tax profit of £20,100, so we deserve to spoil ourselves a little.

Many people will do no more than decide that it all sounds a good idea and 'go for it'. The more careful among us might first negotiate a finance deal on the car and then proceed. Either way, it is often necessary to go to the bank manager to be bailed out with an overdraft, but even with that negotiated it is still sometimes halfway through the year that disaster starts to show itself.

Why? Well let's look at your cash management in more detail. We will start with a simple document. We will divide the paper in two down the page. On the left side we will record all the money that comes in, and on the right we will record all the money that goes out. We shall take the details from your earnings and the expenses we defined in Chapter 3.

Your Personal
CASH ACCOUNT
For the Year Ending 30 Sept 20XX

CASH IN	£	CASH OUT	£
Opening Balance	nil		
Salary	25,000	Travel	650
		Phone Calls	870
		Office Costs	380
		Tax	3,000
Totals	£25,000		£4,900

Accountants don't actually leave their books looking like the above as they 'balance their books'. But in these days of micro-computerized accounting systems there is little to be gained by confusing you with the subtleties of bookkeeping transactions and, risking the wrath of any die-hard accountants who might read this book, we shall leave the cash account in the sensible way shown above.

The cash account shows that you have received a total of £25,000 and you have spent £4,900, thus leaving you with £25,000 less £4,900 = £20,100. So, you could start the next year's account on the left-hand side (showing that to date more money has been received than paid out) with:

Opening balance	£20,100

There now follows a technical description of why money in the bank is on the left side of the bank account (and is thus a debit) and money you owe the bank is listed on the right side of the bank account (and is thus a credit).

If you have studied bookkeeping, or looked over the shoulder of someone entering information in handwritten books, you may have noticed that the left side of the page is headed 'Debits' and the right side of the page is headed 'Credits'. This has been so since the days the books were entered with a quill pen.

In accounting, balances that sit on the left side of a page are called debit balances and those on the right, credit balances. When goods are sold on credit, the value of the invoice is credited to sales on the right side of the page while the customer account is 'debited', hence 'debtors' is used by accountants to signify the balances owed us by our credit customers. When we purchase items the purchase account is entered on the left side whilst our supplier's account is entered on the right, ie it is credited, hence the term 'creditors' is used by accountants to signify suppliers' accounts.

It's just a pity that accountants have not realized that not everyone has entered up the books of account with quill pens and are thus not familiar with the intricacies of debits and credits. The result is mass confusion with more than half the non-financial managers getting the two the wrong way round and thus reversing all the actions the accountants recommend.

If you think this last statement is an exaggeration I can assure you that I have seen it happen in a significant British company with a sales turnover exceeding £2 billion. The more the accountants and chief executive implored their managers to shorten their debtor days and increase their creditor days, the longer their customers took to pay them and the quicker they paid their suppliers. Wouldn't it be a lot easier if we called them 'customer accounts' and 'supplier accounts'?

I hate to describe a situation that may cause even more confusion, but you need to be aware that money sitting or received in our bank or cash account is recorded on the left side of the page while money paid out is recorded on the right side of the page (as can be seen above).

The end result is that money in the bank is a debit balance, while an overdraft is recorded as a credit balance, ie the very opposite way around to the bank statement.

The reason for this is that the bank statement is actually a record of the account in the bank's books. Therefore, if you have money in your account then, in the bank's books, it should show up as the bank owing you money, ie a credit balance in their books but a debit balance in your books.

If you go overdrawn then the bank's books should show you as owing them money, just in the same way as a customer or debtor. In the bank's books, the transaction would therefore be recorded on the left side of the account and you would be shown as a debtor on their statement that they send to you. In your books they would, and must, be the other way round for it to make sense. A debtor in the bank's books is someone who owes the bank money. In your books, if you owe the bank money and are overdrawn then the bank account needs to be listed with the creditors, the people we owe.

Those are the technical reasons for the part of bookkeeping that most confuses students and non-accountants. The easy explanation is that, in your own books of accounts, you need to reverse the bank statement. So, the money in the bank is shown on the left side, and is therefore listed as a *debit* balance, while money you owe the bank, either on a loan or overdraft, is listed on the right side, and is therefore a *credit* balance. Hence:

Debits	£	Credits	£
Opening balance	£20,100		

At this stage the cash account and the profit and loss account give the same results, and this is because we have assumed that you received cash and that you paid all your bills in cash. In real life this may not have been the case. You might not have received all your phone bills, but you might have made an accrual (Chapter 1). In this case, the profit would remain at £20,100, but you would be sitting on more cash (ie the amount of the accrual).

You may have spent money on items that do not occur on the profit and loss account (eg you may have bought a new dining-room suite or a new car). You will be aware from chapters 1 and 2 that items we own are listed on a balance sheet (as are items we owe). Only one year's depreciation appears on the profit and loss account.

The end result is that the cash you have in hand on 30 September 20XX might be very different from the profit that was revealed on your own profit and loss account:

Profit and Loss Account
For Year Ending 30 September 20XX

	£	£
Sale of Services		25,000
Less Direct Costs		650
GROSS PROFIT		24,350
Less Expenses		
Phone Calls	870	
Office Costs	380	
Depreciation	200	1,450
TRADING PROFIT		22,900
Less TAX		3,000
PROFIT after TAX		£19,900

You will see that we have now included depreciation as a heading under expenses on the profit and loss account but, as discussed in chapters 1 and 2, depreciation is just a reduction in the 'book value' and does not involve the movement of cash.

We spent the cash when we purchased the item. For example, suppose we bought a car for £12,000. At that moment the cash was reduced on the balance sheet by £12,000, but the fixed assets increased by £12,000 as the car appeared. That was the total movement of cash.

In following years we reduce the value of the car on the balance sheet to reflect its wear and tear and we 'charge' one year's depreciation against profits. *But we don't involve any cash.*

It's rather like your own car. Unless you drive a vintage model, at the end of a year your motor car is worth less than it was at the beginning of the year. You would thus include it in your year-end balance sheet at the end-of-year valuation. You haven't put any cash on one side to buy another when this one wears out; you have merely written it on the balance sheet at the lower value, and then written the difference in value over that period under expenses on your profit and loss account.

We merely reduce the book value of the car, and reduce that

year's profit by the same amount without putting any cash anywhere.

Depreciation will not, therefore, appear on your cash account. However, all the other items we wish to purchase do, and if we were to detail all the grand plans we have for the year then we might get a very different feeling for what we can really afford:

CASH ACCOUNT
Year Ending 30 September 20XX

CASH IN	£	CASH OUT	£
Opening Balance	nil		
Salary	25,000	Travel	650
Cash from Loan for car	6,000	Phone Calls	660
		Office Costs	380
		Tax	3,000
		Purchase of new car	12,000
		Purchase of new furniture	2,900
		Personal expenses	
		Mortgage	8,000
		Food	5,500
		Clothing	1,600
		Holiday	2,850
		Interest on Loan	720
		Interest on Overdraft	1,099
Totals	31,000		£39,359

You can see from your above 'profit and loss account' that although you made a profit of £19,900 from working in the year ending 30 September 20XX, you have in fact spent much more than that throughout the year. Your spending has been on things that did not appear on your personal profit and loss account and as a result at the end of the year you were in fact overdrawn at the bank by £8,359. Expect a letter from the bank manager any day now.

Without making out such a list you might never have realized just how much cash you need to pay your way through the year.

The items that are commonly missed are the interest on the loan, the overdraft and the repayments on the loan.

Even if we assume that no repayments of the capital amount (£12,000) are required in the first year, your required overdraft still appears to be £8,359.

In the year, you spent more than you received, so your opening balance in your cash account for next year will appear on the cash out side, indicating that more cash has gone out than has come in:

Cash out	£
Opening balance	8,359

This phenomenon of people and companies making a profit and yet still going broke is a common one in business, and in life.

If the above really was your own cash account then you can see that, although you received £25,000 from selling your services (or from your employment) and another £6,000 from a loan (making £31,000 in all), you in fact spent a total of £39,359. You therefore finish the year needing an overdraft of £8,359. There is nothing really wrong with that, providing you have arranged the overdraft in advance and you can afford the interest and repayments on this *and* the loan.

However, a move from borrowings of nil to a total borrowings of £14,359 (£6,000 loan + £8,359 overdraft) in one year on an annual salary (or sales) of £25,000 would seem to be a recipe for trouble.

We realize that the year contained a number of 'one-off' expenditures (eg the car and the dining-room suite). However, if you suffer a downturn in income for whatever reason (short-time working, redundancy, unpaid leave, an unexpected baby or whatever), it may not be possible for you to meet the interest and repayment schedules on your borrowings. Then the troubles would begin.

It is better by far to organize and plan your cash requirements. It may be that, rather than include such heavy capital expenditure (spending on long-term assets such as the car and the furniture) in one year, it would be wiser to buy only one item this year and the other item later, when the loan for the first is repaid or nearly repaid. It may be that the holiday needs to be put back. It may not be as much fun that way but at least you will still have a place to sleep at night and food on the table.

As in all management decisions, there is inevitably more than one way of solving the problem. But the important thing is to solve it before it becomes acute; don't just leave it until you run out of cash.

The *timing* of all expenditure is of vital importance.

Even throughout the year, the timing of expenditure needs to be planned. A monthly (or even weekly) forecast of the cash account is recommended. It really does need to be undertaken at the start of each year and then updated regularly to ensure that you have enough money to meet your cash requirements throughout the year.

Let us assume that at the start of the financial year (ie October 20XX) you're feeling good with a profit of £19,900 behind you and you have got the agreement from your bank, or some other financial institution, to a loan of £6,000 for your car. But they insist upon an overdraft limit of £2,500 throughout the year. On 1 October 20XX you buy a car for £12,000 and order the furniture for £2,900.

By halfway through January things are looking pretty good, so you book your holiday by paying a deposit with the balance due in May, when you are off on holiday to the sun. You buy half your clothing in the January sales and the rest in April, ready for your holiday. Tax is payable in January and September. Your travel to and from work is by rail and you buy an annual season ticket in October.

Without planning you might decide to chance it, especially as you have negotiated a bank overdraft to cover any unexpected fluctuations in fortune. With planning you get a far better picture of the fate that awaits you.

Although a monthly cash flow forecast is recommended, we are going to produce a quarterly cash flow forecast in order to avoid 'drowning' you in figures. Even on a quarterly basis it should give us an indication of where we might expect problems in the forthcoming year:

CASH FLOW FORECAST
For Year Ending 30 September 20XX
(First Draft)

	First Quarter	Second Quarter	Third Quarter	Fourth Quarter	Total Year
Opening Balance	nil	(8,364)	(9,398)	(8,990)	nil
CASH IN					
Salary (Sales)	6,250	6,250	6,250	6,250	25,000
Loan	6,000	–	–	–	6,000
Total Cash In	£12,250	6,250	6,250	6,250	31,000
CASH OUT					
Travel to/from work	650	–	–	–	650
Phone Calls	165	165	165	165	660
Office Costs	100	120	80	80	380
Tax	–	1,500	–	1,500	3,000
Capital Equipment					
Car	12,000	–	–	–	12,000
Furniture	2,900	–	–	–	2,900
Personal Expenses					
Mortgage	2,000	2,000	2,000	2,000	8,000
Food	1,375	1,375	1,375	1,375	5,500
Clothing	1,000	300	300	–	1,600
Holiday	–	1,370	1,480	–	2,850
Interest on Loan	180	180	180	180	720
Sub-total Cash Out	20,370	7,010	5,580	5,300	38,260
Net cash	(8,120)	(9,124)	(8,728)	(8,040)	(7,260)
Interest and Charges	(244)	(274)	(262)	(319)	(1,099)
Closing Balance	(8,364)	(9,398)	(8,990)	(8,359)	(8,359)

Note: the closing balance for each quarter is obtained by adding the opening balance to the total cash in and then deducting the total cash out and the interest. The closing balance at the end of the first quarter must therefore be the opening balance at the start of the second quarter and so on.

A cash flow forecast allows you to plan in advance to avoid problems before a commitment is made. A look at the overdraft level that is required to support this cash flow forecast would indicate that something must go. If you are committed to the purchases of the car and the furniture in the first quarter then it is the holiday and clothing that must suffer if you are to stay within your borrowing limits.

If you plan in advance then you can make sure that you have the cash available to meet your commitments given normal circumstances, even if it means paring those commitments down to the cash that is available. You can 'cut your coat according to your cloth' and spend within your agreed cash limits, instead of waiting for the letter from the bank asking to see you (or worse, bouncing your cheques).

I know you made a good profit (£19,900) and this along with a loan from the bank (£6,000) may have led you to believe you had £25,900 available. So, you could afford the car (£12,000), the furniture (£2,900), a good holiday (£2,850) and new clothes (£1,600), and still have £6,550 in the bank.

Unfortunately *profit* is not *cash*.

Profit is having a business that is worth more at the end of the period than it was at the beginning. Cash is the thing that pays the bills and you do not have enough of it to do all you wish.

It is unfortunate, but within your own cash flow something must go, or at least be delayed. Even though you have borrowed heavily you simply do not have sufficient cash resources to cover all you would like to do.

It is time to be reasonable and prudent, rather than rash and bankrupt. Either the holiday must be delayed, or a more modest car purchased, or the dining suite delayed until you can afford it. It would be more prudent (even though it might be less satisfying) if, in the light of what has been revealed by the cash flow forecast, all three were trimmed.

It may not be such fun with a cheaper car and holiday, and you may have to wait until the end of the year before you can buy your dining-room suite, but at least you sleep at night knowing that you have provided for all the cash you need. You even have a little reserve on the overdraft should you need it.

Successfully 'cutting your coat according to the cloth' and staying out of the clutches of the bankruptcy court would result in something along the lines of:

CASH FLOW FORECAST
For Year Ending 30 September 20XX
(Final Draft)

	First Quarter	Second Quarter	Third Quarter	Fourth Quarter	Total Year
Opening balance	nil	(2,287)	(1,902)	(1,475)	nil
CASH IN					
Salary (sales)	6,250	6,250	6,250	6,250	£25,000
Loan	6,000	–	–	–	6,000
Total Cash In	12,250	6,250	6,250	6,250	31,000
CASH OUT					
Travel to/from work	650	–	–	–	650
Phone Calls	165	165	165	165	660
Office Costs	100	120	80	80	380
Tax	–	1,500	–	1,500	3,000
Capital Equipment					
Car	10,000	–	–	–	10,000
Furniture	–	–	–	1,200	1,200
Personal Expenses					
Mortgage	2,000	2,000	2,000	2,000	8,000
Food	1,375	1,375	1,375	1,375	5,500
Clothing	–	300	300	–	600
Holiday	–	170	1,680	–	1,850
Interest On Loan	180	180	180	180	720
Total Cash Out	14,470	5,810	5,780	6,500	32,560
Net Cash	(2,220)	(1,847)	(1,432)	(1,725)	(1,560)
Interest and Charges	(67)	(55)	(43)	(37)	(202)
Closing Balance	(2,287)	(1,902)	(1,475)	(1,762)	(1,762)

To summarize Chapter 5:

- Cash is the most vital resource of all. Without cash the business cannot pay its workers their wages, it cannot pay its suppliers, or interest on its loans, or the Inland Revenue its dues.
- Profit is the difference in value between the net worth (net asset value) of a company at the beginning of the year and that at the end of that year.

- Cash is the actual money that you have at any one moment, either in your pocket or purse, or in your bank account.
- Cash management is the skill of ensuring that there is always enough cash available to meet the requirement of yourself or your company. Cash management is also the skill of managing the needs of yourself and the company to match the cash resources that can be made available.
- Problems of implementing successful cash management include the cultural barriers that have been set up within each organization, either consciously or unconsciously, and the 'tribal' behaviours within functional management that often make it almost impossible to achieve success from within.
- Most non-financial managers take little or no responsibility for the cash management of the business and just do not understand it.
- The key to success is first to refocus managers to the fundamental importance of cash management, and then to point them in the direction of sound cash management within their own organization. The returns on such a task can be enormous, far beyond the costs.
- The fundamental message that every manager must appreciate is that cash management is the number one responsibility of everyone in the business. Without it, there is no business.
- Depreciation will not appear on your cash account. We merely reduce the book value of the car, and reduce that year's profit by the same amount without putting any cash anywhere.
- This phenomenon of people and companies making a profit and yet still going broke is a common one in business, and in life.
- It is better by far to organize and plan your cash requirements.
- As in all management decisions there is inevitably more than one way of solving the problem. The important thing is to solve it before it becomes acute; don't just leave it until you run out of cash.
- The timing of all expenditure is of vital importance.
- Even throughout the year the timing of expenditure needs to be planned. A monthly (or even weekly) forecast of the cash account is recommended. It really does need to be undertaken at the start of each year and then updated regularly to ensure

that you have enough money to meet your cash requirements throughout the year.

- Without planning you might decide to chance it, especially if you have negotiated a bank overdraft to cover any unexpected fluctuations in fortune. With planning you get a far better picture of the fate that awaits you.
- A cash flow forecast allows you to plan in advance to avoid problems before a commitment is made.
- If you plan in advance then you can make sure that you have the cash available to meet your commitments given normal circumstances, even if it means paring those commitments down to the cash that is available.
- You can 'cut the coat according to the cloth' and spend within your agreed cash limits instead of waiting for the letter from the bank asking to see you (or worse, bouncing your cheques).

If you conquer cash flow, and are aware of the requirements of the profit and loss account and the balance sheet, you can then begin a dialogue with your accountant that might prove to be extremely beneficial to both of you.

6

Cash management and the cash flow statement

Chapter 5 looked in some detail at the importance of managing your cash. If you have turned straight to this chapter then it is recommended that you first read Chapter 5, or at least the summary bullet points.

There is little doubt that good cash management should be part of the psyche of every manager. The old ways of leaving cash management to the accountant are no longer valid in the twenty-first century. Cash management involves you and everyone else in your organization.

In Chapter 5 we looked at a cash account and our plans for the 12 months ahead, which we projected into a cash flow forecast. The cash flow forecast is the means by which we assess how much cash we will require to meet the needs of the organization's plans for the year ahead (or for any other period of time we wish the forecast to cover).

It is often the case that when the plans have been evaluated and their cash requirements discovered (via a cash flow forecast), we find that the company just cannot afford to continue with their original plan unless some modification is made. The whole point of forecasting is to discover and reveal these problems well ahead of time, instead of letting things happen and then discovering too late that you have no cash to meet the obligations, or to pay the wages.

It is now time that we examined a cash flow statement from a published set of accounts contained within a company's annual return:

A Company Ltd
Consolidated **Balance Sheets**

£000s	Notes	This Year	Last Year
Fixed Assets			
Tangible Assets	12	295	290
Investments	13	5	15
		300	305
Current Assets			
Stocks	14	245	225
Debtors	15	275	245
Cash at bank & in hand	16	84	105
		604	575
Current Liabilities			
Bank overdrafts	19	30	25
Other creditors	17	280	260
		310	285
Net Current Assets		**294**	**290**
Total Assets less Current Liabilities		**594**	**595**
Creditors falling due after more than one year			
Other creditors	18	130	135
Convertible debt	18	35	35
		165	170
Provisions for liabilities and charges	20	**65**	**45**
NET ASSETS		**364**	**380**
Capital & Reserves			
Equity share capital	22	60	60
Non-equity share capital	22	5	5
		65	65
Share premium account	23	115	115
Other reserves	23	35	35
Profit & loss account	24	119	135
Shareholders Funds		334	350
Equity minority interests	26	30	30
Total Capital & Reserves		**364**	**380**

A Company Ltd
Consolidated Cash Flow Statement

£000s	Notes	This Year	Last Year
Net Cash Inflow from operating	31	**86.0**	**99.0**
Net Cash Outflow on investments & servicing of finance			
Interest received		6.5	9.5
Interest paid		(19.5)	(27.5)
Dividends received		0.6	0.6
Dividends paid		(22.5)	(20.5)
Dividends paid to minority shareholders		(2.0)	(2.5)
		(36.9)	(40.4)
Tax paid			
UK corporation tax paid		(1.5)	(8.5)
Overseas tax paid		(17.0)	(12.0)
		(18.5)	**(20.5)**
Net Cash Outflow from investing activities			
Purchase of tangible fixed assets		(55.5)	(30.5)
Purchase of subsidiary undertakings	31	(1.0)	(0.5)
Purchase of investments		–	(0.5)
Sale of tangible fixed assets		5.5	11.5
Sale of subsidiary undertakings	31	2.0	17.2
Sale of investments		10.0	3.5
		(39.0)	(0.7)
Net Cash (outflow)/inflow before financing		**(8.4)**	**38.8**
Financing			
Issue of ordinary share capital		–	4.5
Issue of shares to minorities		–	–
Redemption of minorities		–	(4.5)
New long-term loans		5.0	15.5
New short-term loans		34.5	78.5
Issue of convertible loan notes		–	32.5
Repayment of amounts borrowed		(52.3)	(130.5)
Net Cash (outflow)/inflow from financing		**(12.8)**	**(4.0)**
(Decrease)/increase in cash and equivalent		**(21.2)**	**34.8**

£000s	Notes	This Year	Last Year
A Company Ltd Consolidated **Profit and Loss Account**			
Turnover	1&2	**1,150**	**1,085**
Cost of sales	1	(810)	(755)
Gross Profit		**340**	**330**
Distribution costs	1	(185)	(175)
Administration	1	(85)	(80)
Other operating income	1&3	5	5
Operating Income	1,2&3	**75**	**80**
Profit on sale of fixed asset	1	1	6
Loss on sale of operations	1	(28)	–
Profit before Interest	2	**48**	**86**
Share of profits in assoc. companies		1	1
Interest receivable	6	7	10
Interest payable	7	(20)	(30)
Profit before Taxation		**36**	**67**
Tax	8	(18)	(22)
Profit after tax		**18**	**45**
Minority interest		(4)	(5)
Profit for Ordinary Shareholders		**14**	**40**
Dividends	10	(30)	(24)
Transferred to (from) reserves	24	**(16)**	**16**

If you have progressed through the earlier chapters then you should be able to find your way through A Company's balance sheets and the profit and loss accounts without too much trouble. They are slightly abbreviated in detail from the ones we looked at earlier in this book but most of the detail that is missing from the face of these documents can be found in the notes to the accounts that are notated alongside the relevant heading.

We will be examining some of these notes where they are relevant to the cash flow statement, for that is the subject of this chapter. Let us start with the heading:

Consolidated Cash Flow Statement

The term 'consolidated' is used to denote that the account or statement is the amalgam or consolidation of the accounts of the company plus all the subsidiary companies and organizations it owns and/or controls.

In published accounts there are usually two years' results displayed and each year is usually given a date to identify it but, to keep matters relevant to today, I have used 'This Year' and 'Last Year'.

Net Cash Inflow from Operating Activities 31 86.0 99.0

This is taken from the operating profit of the company (as shown on the profit and loss account), which is then adjusted for 'non-cash' items, eg depreciation. To see how the accountant moved from the figure shown as operating profit in the profit and loss account (£75,000) to that shown on the cash flow statement (£86,000) we need to look at the notes that are given alongside this item.

The profit and loss account described the profit as operating income instead of operating profit for all the reasons given on page 46 (NB the neat change of title in Note 31 where the same item becomes the operating profit. It is also sometimes described as trading profit, PBIT, profit from operations and so on.)

Note 31	This Year	Last Year
Operating profit	75.0	80.0
Depreciation	45.1	41.1
(Increase) /decrease in stocks	(20.0)	5.3
(Increase) /decrease in debtors	(30.0)	(5.4)
(Decrease) /increase in creditors	20.0	0.4
Other non-cash movements	3.9	1.9
Net cash inflow from normal operating activities	94.0	123.3
Net cash outflow from reorganization	(8.0)	(24.3)
Net cash inflow from operating activities	**86.0**	**99.0**

In order to understand Note 31, let's start with the operating profit. If, for the sake of this explanation, we make the assumption that all dealings throughout the year were in cash, and no credit was taken or given, then the operating profit would represent a cash difference between our incomings and outgoings.

If we only dealt in cash then we would have received cash for all our sales in the year and we would then have paid all our suppliers cash, as well as our workers and expenses.

If that was the case and you take the sales, deduct the cost of sales and all the trading expenses, you get the operating profit, which would be all cash. So, by starting the document with the operating profit, we are saved the effort of listing all the individual revenue and costs that made it up. These details are available on the profit and loss account.

We now need to adjust the operating profit for the items it contained that were not dealt with on a total cash basis. We thus start with the operating profit and then add back the non-cash items.

The profit and loss account will have included depreciation among the expenses and, as we discussed in chapters 1 and 2, depreciation does not involve the setting on one side, or the expenditure, of any cash. It is merely a book entry reducing the value of an asset over its lifetime. As we are now looking at the flow of funds, we must add back any non-cash deductions like depreciation that we made on the profit and loss account. We need to think of how movements in the items that make up working capital effect the cash flow statement:

(Increase)/decrease in stocks	(20.0)	5.3
(Increase)/decrease in debtors	(30.0)	(5.4)
(Decrease)/increase in creditors	20.0	0.4

The profit and loss account only contains the costs of the materials used in actual production. If you increase your stocks it does not increase the costs shown on the profit and loss account, but it does increase the value of the asset called stock on the balance sheet. (In the example below, the second column is used to illustrate the effect of suddenly buying a great deal more stock). You will note that the charge to the profit and loss account does not change, but the balance sheet listing of everything we own will increase because we now have more stock in our warehouse. For example, the profit and loss account contains:

e.g. the Profit and Loss account contains –	Actual	Illustration
Opening stock	225	225
+ Purchases	500	**600**
= Stock available for manufacture	725	825
– Closing stock	245	**345**
= Stock used in manufacture	480	480
(and thus charged to the Profit and Loss account)		

If we have more stock then, obviously, we have to pay someone for it. So, on our cash flow statement, our profit from operations is adjusted to reflect that the increase in this year's stock has cost A Company £20,000 (whereas in the previous year the stock reduction had decreased the need to fund it by £5,300):

	This Year	Last Year
(Increase)/decrease in stocks	(20.0)	5.3

We may not have paid our suppliers yet, but there is no doubt that increasing stocks creates a need to increase our funding requirement to pay for it.

The profit and loss account is generally compiled on an accruals basis (see chapters 3 and 4). The profit and loss account is therefore not the least interested in how long you give customers to pay because the sales shown on it are the invoiced sales for the period.

If you allow your customers longer to pay, you clearly will not have that money (in this case £30,000) in your bank account because it will still be in theirs. This costs you cash to replace the 'missing' money, hence:

(Increase)/decrease in debtors	(30.0)	(5.4)

If, on the other hand, you delay paying your suppliers then you have their money (£20,000) in your account hence:

(Decrease) /increase in creditors	20.0	0.4
Once you have included any other non-cash items		
Other non-cash movements	3.9	1.9
You discover the		
Net cash inflow from normal operating activities	94.0	123.3

There are certain non-recurring costs that companies like to show separately and reorganization costs are such an item.

Companies like to show *reorganization costs* under a separate heading as it can then be emphasized that they are non-recurring items. They can be dressed up to look as though they are the result of good positive management action instead of correcting some appalling gaffes that the management made in the past (as is usually the case). Note 31 included this entry:

Net cash outflow from reorganization	(8.0)	(24.3)

As soon as all the adjustments have been completed for the non-cash items that affected our operating profit (income) then we should arrive at the figure shown on the cash flow statement as

Net cash inflow from operating activities	**86.0**	**99.0**

Having covered the effect on cash from our operating activities (which generated £86,000 cash this year in A Company Ltd) we look at what other activities the company got up to in order to generate even more cash:

Net cash outflow on investments & servicing of finance		
Interest received	6.5	9.5
Interest paid	(19.5)	(27.5)
Dividends received	0.6	0.6
Dividends paid	(22.5)	(20.5)
Dividends paid to minority shareholders	(2.0)	(2.5)
	(36.9)	**(40.4)**

The above figures should be able to be reconciled to the differences in the balance sheet at both the start and the end of the year. I should, however, take a moment to explain minority shareholders.

Minority shareholders generally occur when a company takes over another or forms a joint venture and leaves some of the original shareholders intact rather than buying out 100 per cent of the shares.

The reasons for not acquiring all of the shares are varied and it maybe that leaving some of the original shareholders with a minority shareholding intact may lock them into the company, or it may be the only way to gain control of a strategic acquisition. The end result is that, when consolidating accounts, not all of the profit belongs to the shareholders on the controlling company; some belongs to the minority of shareholders who still hold shares in subsidiary companies, hence:

Dividends paid to minority shareholders	(2.0)	(2.5)
Thus		
Net cash outflow on investments and servicing of finance	**(36.9)**	**(40.4)**

The tax paid will differ from the amount of tax shown on the profit and loss due to the time delays between assessing the tax (which you do at the end of the financial year) and paying the tax (which you do in the following year). The cash flow statement contains the actual cash paid, so some could be for this year (advanced corporation tax), some for last year (corporation tax) and some that has been deferred for many years.

Tax paid		
UK corporation tax paid	(1.5)	(6.5)
Overseas tax paid	(17.0)	(12.0)
	(18.5)	**(18.5)**

Next, we account for the *cash* that flowed in or out of the company as a result of our investing activities:

Net cash outflow from investing activities			
Purchase of tangible fixed assets		(55.5)	(30.5)
Purchase of subsidiary undertakings	31	(1.0)	(0.5)
Purchase of investments		–	(0.5)
Sale of tangible fixed assets		5.5	11.5
Sale of subsidiary undertakings	31	2.0	17.2
Sale of investments		10.0	3.5
		(39.0)	(12.0)

The above figures can be reconciled to the differences in the balance sheet at both the start and the end of the year apart, perhaps, for the reasons why the net increase in fixed assets is greater than the difference in the balance sheet values.

The increase on the balance sheet between tangible assets at the beginning and end of the year is £5,000 (£295 – £290) but the net increase in fixed assets bought and sold on the cash flow statement is £50,000 (£55 – £5). Where did the other £45,000 go?

The answer probably lies somewhere in the area of depreciation. If you look at the adjustment to the operating profit for non-cash items you will see that the profit and loss account carried a 'charge' of £45,100 for depreciation to reflect one year's wear and tear on the fixed assets of the company. By the end of that year the tangible assets would have reduced in value by £41,500.

To reflect the increase in value shown in the balance sheet you need to reduce the assets you had at the start of the year by the amount of depreciation that is shown in the profit and loss account. You then subtract from the resultant value the items you have sold, and add on those you have bought, to arrive at an end-of-year valuation.

Thus:

Tangible assets at the start of the year	£290,000
less depreciation for year	(45,100)
less assets sold	(5,500)
add assets purchased	55,500
= Tangible assets at end of the year	£294,900

And so we arrive at a sub-total of all the *cash* items we have covered so far:

Net cash (outflow)/inflow before financing	**(8.4)**	**38.8**

You can see that the management of the company has managed to use up all £86,000 cash that was produced from operations this year and we are left with minus (£8,400) at this stage.

We now need to cover the net cash (outflow)/inflow from financing:

Financing		
Issue of ordinary share capital	–	4.5
Issue of shares to minorities	–	–
Redemption of minorities	–	(4.5)
New long term loans	5.0	15.5
New short-term loans	34.5	78.5
Issue of convertible loan notes	–	32.5
Repayment of amounts borrowed	(52.3)	(130.5)
Net cash (outflow)/inflow from financing	(12.8)	(4.0)

I often get questioned as to why a company would repay loans while it still needs to borrow (as can be seen above). Why doesn't it just reduce or increase its borrowings? One of the main reasons is because of the complexity of the finance instruments there are in today's world.

Companies wish to borrow in the cheapest way possible and will often enter fixed-term agreements. They sometimes offer to convert the lender's loan into shares at a predetermined price on a predetermined date, or enter into one of the vast number of variations to this theme.

The attraction to the person lending them the money is easy to see. If they believe that at redemption the share price will be well above the value of the loan then they might offer the loan at considerably lower interest rates in return for the option to convert into shares.

There are all sorts of fixed dates for repayments of loans and, when they occur, many companies find that they just do not have the cash available to repay them and so are forced into new long- and/or short-term loans to cover their cash requirements. This is another reminder of how important cash is to a business.

The result of all the management activities is:

(Decrease)/increase in cash & equivalent	(21.2)	34.8

They've used up all the money and our bank account is £21,200 the poorer!

The answer as to whether you consider that good or bad is subjective and is for you to work out after you have read Chapter 9. In the meantime, we should consider a few of the other areas of cash management that have confused so many of the non-finance managers in the past.

Working capital

Working capital is a title given to the amount of cash tied up in current assets less current liabilities and it challenges reserves as the most misleading of the accountants' titles.

Throughout all the parts of the world I have worked, including some of the most sophisticated of the western world's companies and organizations, there is an almost universal belief that it is a good thing to have plenty of 'working capital'.

Working capital consists mainly of stock (inventory), debtors (people who owe us money) and cash, less creditors (people to whom we owe money), taxation, dividends owed and other short-term borrowings.

Its title of working capital immediately conjures up the picture of increasing your capital and making it work for you; all excellent virtues.

To increase your working capital you can increase the amount of stock you have on the shelf, increase the number and/or the amount that people owe you and decrease the money you owe.

For years we have been taught that we must have plenty of working capital and at least twice as much value in current assets as we owe in current liabilities. Such a ratio makes accountancy teachers happy, examiners happy and bankers very happy. It seems that everyone is happy – or are they? I certainly am not!

I defy anyone to tell me how stock on the shelf is working for me. It deteriorates, becomes obsolete or past its sell-by date, or it 'walks' out of the store, and what remains needs dusting and counting regularly, thus pushing up the overhead costs of the company.

Many people have pointed out to me that their companies have made huge profits by buying in bulk or ahead of price rises. I cannot and would not dispute their arguments but point out that most companies exist to manufacture or supply their customer base. They are not expert brokers playing the 'futures' market. If they would like to get involved in that market then let's pack up the manufacturing and go into futures – it's a specialist field.

I know of many companies that were kept afloat by stock profits rather than by manufacturing profits. They are the ones that generally collapsed as soon as inflation flattened out.

If they want to include a dabble in the futures market that is fine and its their choice, but there are not many production or stock handlers that know the implications of the futures markets well enough to risk the company's money. Even the finest experts in the world get it wrong. More than one bank has been brought to its knees when gambling its customers' deposits on the futures markets, usually because of the mistakes made by its futures 'experts', and many more will go the same way.

Companies buy in bulk in order to beat a price increase, or to secure volume discounts. However, it is very seldom that the savings made by buying in bulk are greater than the increased costs of holding the stock, shelving it, guarding it, counting it and then, in a year or so (or when its past its sell-by date), writing a load off as obsolete. In addition, most companies need to borrow the money to afford the extra stock, so the interest on the stock value needs to be added to the cost of increased stocks before claiming that a profit has been made from bulk-buying or stocking up ahead of a price increase.

I am also totally perplexed as to why having lots of people owing you money is better than having lots of people who have just paid you. Trade creditors (our suppliers) normally fail to charge interest on overdue accounts, so I cannot see the advantages of rushing to pay them when I can use their money at nil interest rather than borrow from the bank at whatever interest and charges they wish to impose.

Working capital should therefore be nil or, even better, it should be *negative*.

It is interesting to note that, far from harming your profits as many people fear, negative working capital, properly achieved, increases profits and enhances the efficiency and quality of the organization.

Sadly, many academic courses are still teaching its students that you should have twice the value in current assets that you have in current liabilities (the 2:~1 ratio). No wonder banks make so much profit with so little risk.

You can go a long way towards achieving negative working capital without dramatically changing your systems of production and working. Keep an open mind and a close watch on inventory levels – and work out how little support stock you really need (and how much money reducing stock levels would generate). You will see why effective cash management needs everyone to be involved. Stocks are not controlled by the accountant but by production and stores management.

Increase stocks by a day and how much more cash must you find to keep the company going? Decrease stocks by a day and how much cash will you generate to pay your bills or to use elsewhere in the business? (You will be able to answer this for yourself after reading Chapter 9).

Debtors (customers' accounts) is another area vital to the financial health of the company. Where a company is expanding and increasing sales turnover each year it often forgets that it needs more money to 'support' its debtors.

Sales personnel seldom want to upset their customers by pushing them for payment, and thus their customers seldom pay until the debt is very old. In the UK, the average credit period given by suppliers is 30 days or less, whereas the average time taken by their customers to pay their bills is 45 days or more (sometimes considerably more!). Therefore, most customers are getting at least 15 days' free credit from their suppliers. So, with the banks charging a monthly interest on borrowed cash, you can see that if you allow your customers more time than is necessary to pay then you have already begun to wipe out some of your profit margin.

'Debtors' is another area of vital cash management that is not in the accountant's hands, but in the hands of the sales department. They are the ones who set up the deal. If only they would make the collection of cash part of their responsibility they could inject considerable funds into their own companies.

It follows logically from the above that a company's creditors (its suppliers) are also looked upon as a 'source of finance'. A source, furthermore, that is interest-free.

A lot of managers take issue on this point and tell me that there is no such thing as free interest: the interest charge is hidden in the sales price charged by the supplier. When I ask how many of them use suppliers whose prices are higher by the 1 or 2 per cent needed to cover interest, I get no takers. More to the point, when I ask them how many of them increase their prices to their customers to account for the interest on late payments, again no takers. The usual reply is that in the competitive environment of today there just isn't scope in the pricing to add 1 or 2 per cent.

It is little wonder, therefore, that accountants use creditors as a source of interest-free finance, and thus continually extend the time they take to pay them.

While reflecting on the accountants' craft, we should also look at another area that vitally concerns the cash flow of a business:

Foreign exchange

Exchange rates are extremely volatile at the best of times, and if you dabble in this area then you could be playing with fire.

Many companies are tempted (and many fall for the temptation) to borrow overseas as it is possible to raise money at much lower interest rates abroad. However, if the exchange rates move against them it costs far more when they come to repay the debt than the savings they made on the difference in the interest rates in the first place. Indeed, many companies have burnt their fingers so badly on exchange rates that many heads have rolled as a result of exchange losses. The only thing that is certain is that many more will do so in the future.

There are many financial instruments that help to prevent exchange losses, including forward buying, options and hedging, netting and matching, credit guarantees, letters of credit, call and put options… and a multitude of others will no doubt be created in the future.

International currency exchange is of such volatility that the one thing I have learnt is to leave it to the real experts and let them make a real hash of it, for very few people walk away with long-lasting success from this area of cash management.

Most companies have enough to do with managing their core

business (ie the things that are basic to the business, that they understand and that actually makes them a living) without diverging into a world of exchange rates that is a veritable mine-field. Just read the newspapers and note the number of top exec-utives forced to resign for being responsible for their company losing hundreds of millions of pounds or dollars on the exchange markets, thus wiping out many years of work (if not the company itself). I am sure you will be well content to leave the exchange market to the foreign exchange 'experts'.

Net inflow (outflow) from acquisitions and disposals

'Acquisitions' refer to the buying or takeover of companies, whereas 'disposals' refer to the selling off of companies, or parts of a group.

The 1980s was the great era for acquisition growth and we will see it return every decade or so. It is therefore somewhat sobering to read that only about 30 per cent of acquisitions proved to be successful. A lot depends on how you measure success, but there is little doubt that many unsuccessful acquisitions were hidden by the then British method of writing off the goodwill against the reserves.

Most acquisitions, however unsuccessful they are in achieving a satisfactory return on the cost of that acquisition, will neverthe-less boost the 'bottom line'. If they are bought from borrowed cash they will give a higher earnings per share (Chapter 9) to the shareholders. This is because the purchase of the acquisition, and thus the extra profits (another set of profits added to yours will boost the bottom line on the profit and loss account), was made with cash that disappears from the balance sheet, or with paper that appears among the shareholders' funds.

Treat acquisitions with great care, however attractive or strategic they appear. They remind me of the old rule of thumb I used to use on multi-million dollar projects – reckon that it is going to cost twice as much and take twice as long as everyone assures you.

The most successful acquisitions I have seen are those purchased with the cash generated from the successful manage-ment of negative working capital.

If you can then introduce the same sound cash management techniques and principles into your recently acquired company you can recover a great proportion of the costs of that acquisition and so cut the risk factor of failure to a minimum. This will also give you every chance of achieving outstanding returns on your investment, which, at the end of the day, is the name of the game and the reason most people invest their money in a trading organization.

To return to our cash flow statement:

(Decrease)/increase in cash & equivalent	(21.2)	34.8

They've used up all the money generated from the hard work of the company, and then a bit more, so our bank account is now £21,200 the poorer.

Is that bad or good – should we be worried? Again, we must wait until Chapter 9 before we can begin to measure the acceptable level of debt. It is also in that chapter that we will be looking at ways of measuring whether the company could have helped itself a little more by better control of its working capital (stock, debtors and creditors).

In the meantime, it is sufficient for you to be aware of just how much you can learn about a company's cash management from its cash flow statement.

If your regular management reports do not contain a cash flow statement then insist on receiving one that is reconciled to the opening and closing balance sheets. It may save the entire future of your company.

I hope that this has convinced you that cash management not only involves you but also that it is far too important to be left to the accountants!

7

Let's get it all together

In chapters 1 to 6, we have dealt in some detail with the balance sheet, the profit and loss account, the cash account, the cash flow forecast and the cash flow statement. These are the foundation stones upon which accounting is reported.

It is essential that the contents of these accounting statements are understood before we try to form judgements based upon them, or attempt to interpret the financial performance of a company, an organization or any internal division or department.

In the earlier chapters we have concentrated on the three major financial documents and you should by now begin to get the feel of each of them and of their contents. Let us now summarize the main points of all these documents:

Balance sheet

- Lists all we *own* that has a monetary value, and all we *owe* that has a monetary value.
- Subtracts one from the other to give us the net asset value (net worth).
- It also lists the shareholders' funds to reveal the amount of value that the owners have put into the company.
- Total shareholders' funds will always equal the net asset value.
- Total shareholders' funds plus long-term liabilities equals the capital employed.
- Total assets less current liabilities also equal the capital employed.

Profit and loss account

- Is the earnings statement of the company.
- Shows the company's income from (invoiced) sales.
- Deducts all the running costs of the company.
- Sales less the direct costs gives gross profit.
- Gross profit less the overheads gives operating (trading) profit (PBIT).
- Operating profit plus/less interest gives pre-tax profit.
- Pre-tax profit less tax gives after-tax profit (shareholders' return).
- After-tax profit less dividends gives retained profit.
- Add retained profits from previous years to give revenue reserve (shown on the balance sheet).

Cash account

- Records all the movements of cash in and out of the company's bank accounts.
- Starts with the opening balance (last year's closing balance).
- Adds all the cash received from any source.
- Subtracts the cash paid out to any source.
- Opening balance + cash in − cash out = closing balance.
- Cash received is recorded as a debit.
- Cash paid out is recorded as a credit.

Cash flow forecast

- Is the forecast of the cash account over a period ahead.
- In business it is usual to produce a monthly cash flow forecast for the 12 months ahead, but in reality cash is managed on a daily basis (sometimes quite desperately!).
- The cash flow forecast is used to match the cash resources to the requirements of the business and/or match the requirements of the business to the cash that can be made available.

Cash flow statement

Adjusts the operating profit for non-cash items to reveal:

- Net cash inflow (outflow) from operating activities.
- Net cash inflow (outflow) on investments and servicing of finance.
- Net cash inflow (outflow) from investing activities

to reveal:

- Net cash inflow (outflow) before financing.

It then shows the

- Net cash inflow (outflow) from financing

to reveal:

- Increase (decrease) in cash and cash equivalents.

We will now progress and look at how these principal documents can be used in real life. Let's see if we can help John Nephew.

Nephew Ltd

John Nephew's dear old Aunt Agatha has finally quit this life and remembered 'young' John in her will. She has left him some cash and some deposits she had in a couple of banks and a building society. John had always been fond of the old lady in her lifetime and was delighted at her kindness and generosity in the way she had remembered him in her will.

He spent the cash on a meal for his wife and himself at which they toasted the memory of dear Aunt Agatha. They followed the meal with a visit to the theatre and a short break during which he decided what he was going to do with the deposits. With the bank deposits and the amount in the building society he and Mrs Nephew decided to form their own business, manufacturing and selling children's toys.

The total sums on the deposits that had been left to him amounted to £80,000. On 1 January 20XX they formed a limited company, with just his wife and himself as shareholders, named Nephew Ltd. He paid all the deposits into the company's bank account and it became the share capital as he issued 80,000 ordinary shares, 50,000 to himself and the rest to his wife.

His first year was very busy and he worked very hard to get the business off to a good start. He was a talented salesman and with invoiced sales at £960,000, against purchases of goods of £720,000, including an accrual that he had made for invoices received after the year-end, he was feeling pleased with himself as he came to the end of his first year of trading.

The company had collected VAT (sales tax) on its sales and paid VAT on its purchases. All the money collected had been paid to Customs and Excise apart from £1,000 that the company had collected in the last quarter but not yet paid over. He had been told that his accounts should be presented with all figures shown in the same way as he had described his sales and purchases (ie excluding VAT) and all the figures quoted are exclusive of VAT.

At the start of the year he had borrowed £100,000 from a bank at an interest of 12 per cent per annum, with the capital sum (£100,000) repayable in equal instalments at the end of each of the next ten years. He had talked to the bank manager about an overdraft and had an agreement for an overdraft limit of £50,000 to cover 'the company's day-to-day needs' at an overdraft rate of 18 per cent per annum. Any money on deposit would receive interest at 8 per cent.

The company had purchased, and paid for, a seven-year lease on business premises for £140,000, and some plant and equipment for £50,000. He was hoping that the plant and equipment would last him ten years. He bought two second-hand vehicles for the business, which had cost a total of £15,000 and should last him three years, when he would hope to sell them for a total of £3,000.

At the end of his first year he thought it had been such a good start to the business that he would pay the shareholders (himself and his wife) a dividend of 10 per cent, and was therefore considering the worth of his company.

He looked around the stores and estimated that he had about £48,000 worth of stock at year-end, although a batch that had cost £8,000 was faulty and couldn't be used. Unfortunately he couldn't return it as the supplier had gone bust.

During the year he had employed four people working in production at a total cost of £30,000 and also incurred another £1,610 of production overheads.

Fuel and delivery costs were a further £40,000. Selling and advertising had cost him £56,000, although that sum included a cost (£3,000) for a holiday that he and Mrs Nephew had enjoyed and that had been booked through the company. Administration had cost £8,000 and he paid himself and Mrs Nephew a wage of £1,000 a month each.

He enjoyed a good relationship with his customers and his terms of trade were for payment in 30 days. In fact, his debtors at the end of his first year on 31 December 20XX were £240,000.

He had settled all the suppliers' invoices he had received by the year-end and all the service invoices. The staff were paid up to date.

He knew of approximately £60,000 worth of suppliers' invoices that would not be arriving until after the year-end for goods that he had received before the end of the year, most of which were still in stock.

He must pay 42 per cent tax on profits and understood that the capital allowances would work out approximately the same as depreciation, so he could ignore any adjustment of profits and calculate tax on the pre-tax profits shown on a profit and loss account. Not being an accountant, he didn't really understand what that meant, but he nodded wisely and knowingly when he heard about it.

His first year had seemed to him to progress excellently and the success of his first venture into business had allowed him to enjoy a splendid Christmas. He returned to his office on 1 January 20XX to deal with the mail that had piled up over the Christmas break and to catch up with paying some of his suppliers. He felt good about life in general and the business in particular as he opened the first letter. It was from his bank manager.

'… I am extremely worried about the size of your overdraft. It is way beyond anything we agreed… The situation is critical… It is essential that you don't issue any more cheques… Please make an immediate appointment… '

The tone of the letter shocked and worried John Nephew considerably. He had been confident that the business was doing very well. His feelings of goodwill towards all men evaporated rapidly, and his spirits sank into his boots with an audible thump.

He'd always kept his own personal bank account separate from that of the business. He kept an eye on the balance in his own account, leaving the business bank account to look after itself. He reasoned that, provided he was selling at a profit and at a sales margin that covered all his overheads and expenses, his business bank account must be all right.

He was confident that he hadn't made any mistakes on his pricing and he had used all his energies to concentrate on selling and managing the bottom line. He reasoned that if he did that then everyone should be happy and the business should enjoy good profits.

'So what is this aggro from the bank manager at a time like this?' he muttered to himself. 'I really don't like the tone of this letter one little bit. I'd no idea that we had a serious problem with the bank, yet this all sounds deadly serious! What do I do if the bank manager takes drastic action and stops the company's cheques? We'll go out of business. What the devil can I do?'

John began to worry. He had never really understood finance and before setting up his own business, when he had been a line manager, he had just nodded in what he hoped were the right places when the accountant spoke. He had always been able to flannel his way through when finance was discussed. Now, according to his bank manager, he was facing an apparent financial crisis that couldn't just be 'nodded' away.

All the insecurity caused by his lack of financial knowledge started to show and he began to pace around his office as he could feel the rapid build-up of stress, if not panic. He clenched his fists until the knuckles showed white. The hairs on his neck stood on end and he began to perspire.

What on earth could have gone wrong? He was certain that all his calculations of profit margins were correct and that he was making profits. His previous company had been expert at managing the bottom line and he had been one of its most effective managers. What can the bank manager be worried about?

On 1 January 20XX it is not easy to contact anyone at work (and sober), let alone willing to take on an immediate crisis such as the one John Nephew was facing and, after a number of phone calls, all to no avail, he was beginning to despair. There was a leaden feeling in the pit of his stomach.

Suddenly, at the darkest moment, a light shone in his mind. He felt inspired, all was not lost; there was someone who might just be able to help him. He's just thought of you.

He remembers you saying that you are halfway through reading a book on how to master finance. The relief floods through his body as he picks up the phone, and pours the whole story out to you.

You listen to him patiently, unable to interrupt until he finally finishes and pauses for breath. You think quickly, considering what you can do to help, or even if you can help him in his predicament.

He has an imminent appointment with his bank manager and asks if you can use the knowledge you have acquired so far to produce anything that might help him. You then ask him for a few moments to think about his predicament, put the phone down, sit back, and consider.

You realize that he urgently needs, at the very least, a cash account, a cash flow statement, a profit and loss account and a balance sheet.

You have read in the earlier chapters of this book all the rules and hints concerning the construction of all four documents and you feel that you just might be able to put these four accounting documents together for John Nephew.

You realize that its Nephew's first year of trading and any profit he makes will show up at the bottom of the profit and loss account. Any money that's left after paying the shareholders a dividend will also become the revenue reserve (retained profits) on the bottom of the balance sheet. So far, so good.

You also realize that you know how to produce a cash account and that, as it is now past the end of his first year, there is no point in producing a forecast of monthly or quarterly cash flow over that year. All you need is the cash account, either in the two halves of the page as we did earlier, or vertically down the page (cash in on the top half, cash out on the bottom half).

The closing balance on that cash account will become the figure you will show as cash under the current assets on the balance sheet, or, if the business proves to be overdrawn, then it will appear as bank overdraft under the current liabilities.

You decide that you have nothing to lose by having a go and pick up the phone to John Nephew to tell him:

'I'm not an accountant and I don't pretend to be one. I don't feel that I can accept any responsibility for any errors I might make, but if that's acceptable to you then I am prepared to have a go at producing some accounts that may enable you to talk finance with your bank manager.'

John Nephew is overjoyed and asks you to start straight away

– there is no time to lose. You tell him that you understand that a limited company's accounts must be audited and he must realize that there is no way that you are acting in that capacity. However, as a friend, you'll do all you can to help. He fully understands and agrees.

You think about the task ahead. It is clear to you that Nephew Ltd needs a balance sheet and a profit and loss account. You must also produce a cash account to work out how much money he has had in and how much he has spent out.

You get three sheets of paper (A4 or quarto size) and on each you write the heading and titles appropriate to one of the three documents. Once that is completed you realize that you have a format that will not only help you in this task, but also one that you can use over and over again. You copy the layout of the accounts that was included in the earlier chapters of this book.

Your sheets of paper should look similar to those on the next few pages and, if you really want to master finance, it is strongly recommended that you try this exercise for yourself.

What we are about to do is to take all the facts that John Nephew has given us in the story above and put them together into the financial documents. If you have read the earlier chapters then you should by now be able to have a good try at completing the cash account and filling in most of the balance sheet and the profit and loss account. If you handle everything correctly then the balance sheet will actually balance at the end of the exercise.

We have given you a blank copy of the three key documents you need for this exercise and we recommend that you copy them on to A4 sheets. If you decide to write directly on to the blank formats within this book then make sure you use a soft pencil and have a soft eraser handy – very few people get it completely correct at the first time of trying.

We have also taken the opportunity to gather all the blank formats together in this chapter. So you will find a format for the 'cash flow statement', as discussed in Chapter 6, but this may be ignored for the moment by those who are reading just the odd-numbered chapters.

You might find it easiest if you start with the cash account, then the profit and loss account and then the balance sheet. However, you learn the most if you try to complete all three sheets at the same time.

Look at each point in the story of John Nephew and decide on which of the sheets each value should go (it may go on more than one).

First, the formats:

Name (eg Nephew Ltd)
CASH ACCOUNT
For the Year Ending

Total £ in Year

Opening Balance
CASH IN during the year
  Sales
    plus Opening Trade Debtors
    less Closing Trade Debtors   (_____)
  Non-Trade Debtors (Increase) Decrease
  Sale of Fixed Assets
  Issue of Shares
  New Medium & Long Term Loans
  Interest Received
  Cash from Investments
  Disposals of Companies
  Cash from other sources
  Total Cash Available   £
    (Opening Balance + Cash In)

CASH OUT during the year
  Purchases   ( )
    plus Opening Trade Creditors ( )
    less Closing Trade Creditors _____ ( )
  Non-Trade Creditors Increase (Decrease)
  Employee Costs   ( )
  Premises Costs   ( )
  Interest Paid   ( )
  Tax Paid   ( )
  Dividends Paid   ( )
  Capital Equipment (Fixed Assets) Purchased ( )
  Acquisitions   ( )
  Investments   ( )
  Loan Repayments   ( )
  Other Cash Expenditure   ( )
  Sub-total Cash Out   £ (_____)
Net Cash at Bank or (Overdrawn)
  Interest on Overdraft   ( )
  Closing Balance   £ _____

Name
Profit and Loss Account
<u>For the Year Ending</u>

Sales   £   £
 Less <u>COST OF GOODS SOLD</u>
  Materials*   (   )
  Direct Labour   (   )
  Factory Expenses   (_____) (_____)

GROSS PROFIT   £
 Less <u>OVERHEADS</u> (Indirect Expenses)
  Production indirect expenses (   )
  Sales & Marketing   (   )
  Delivery   (   )
  Premises   (   )
  Administration   (   )
  Other Operating Expenses (_____) (_____)

OPERATING (TRADING) PROFIT (PBIT)   £
 Interest   (_____)

PRE-TAX PROFITS   £
 Taxation   (   )

AFTER-TAX PROFITS   £
 Interim Dividend (paid)   (   )
 Final Dividend (proposed) (_____) (_____)

RETAINED PROFITS for the Year   £
 add Retained Profits for Previous Years

<u>Total Retained Profits (REVENUE RESERVE)</u>   £

*Materials = Opening Stock
plus Purchases _____
= Total Materials available for Sale
less Closing Stock (_____)
= <u>Materials charged to COST OF GOODS SOLD</u> £ _____

Name
Balance Sheet as at

	£ cost	£ depn	£ value
Fixed Assets			
Land & Buildings			
Plant & Equipment			
Vehicles	———	———	———
	£	£	£
Investments			£
Intangible Assets			£

Current Assets
Stock
Debtors
Cash ————— £

Current Liabilities
Creditors ( )
Bank Overdraft ( )
Taxation ( )
Proposed Dividends (————) £( )
Net Current Assets
(Current Assets less Current Liabilities) £

Capital Employed
(Total Assets less Short-term Liabilities) £

Long-term Liabilities
Loans ( )
Debenture ( )
Mortgage (————) ( )

Net Asset Value £

Shareholders' Funds
Ordinary Shares
Preference Shares
Capital Reserve
Revenue Reserve
Total Shareholders Funds £

Name
Cash Flow Statement for period

£	Notes	This Year	Last Year
Net cash inflow(outflow) from operating activities			
Net cash inflow(outflow) on investments and servicing of finance			
Interest received			
Interest paid			
Dividends received			
Dividends paid			
Dividends paid to minority shareholders			
		£	£
Net tax inflow(outflow) from taxation			
UK corporation tax paid			
Overseas tax paid			
		£	£
Net cash inflow(outflow) from investing activities			
Purchase of tangible fixed assets			
Purchase of subsidiary undertakings			
Purchase of investments			
Sale of tangible fixed assets			
Sale of subsidiary undertakings			
Sale of investments			
		£	£
Net cash inflow(outflow) before financing		**£**	**£**
Financing			
Net cash inflow(outflow) from financing activities			
Issue of ordinary share capital			
Issue of shares to minorities			
Redemption of minorities			
New long-term loans			
New short-term loans			
Issue of convertible loan notes			
Repayment of amounts borrowed			
Net cash inflow(outflow) from financing			
Increase(Decrease) in cash and equivalent		**£**	**£**

If you've copied out the formats on to your blank sheets of A4 then you're ready to go. If you've read the earlier chapters then you may be surprised by how much you can successfully complete without reading the next few pages.

It will be a great challenge for you to see if you can complete your blank formatted account documents for Nephew Ltd before you read on past this line and a great learning curve will have been ascended.

Don't worry about making a mistake; you can always make out another blank format and try again. It's the learning you will have achieved in trying that is important.

If at the end of all your entries the balance sheet fails to balance, you are probably in good company: 90 per cent of readers will have left out or missed one small detail and that will prevent it balancing even if 99 per cent is correct. (I know a lot of accountants who qualified after more than 5 years of exams without once successfully balancing their balance sheet in any exam!)

If you're going to have a go at the accounts documents of Nephew Ltd on your own, now is the time. The following pages start the transfer of the details into the books of account.

If you're uncertain what to do next, let's consider the first relevant paragraph of John Nephew's story. Let us remind ourselves of the information given.

'The total sums on the deposits that had been left to him amounted to £80,000. On 1 January 20XX they formed a limited company with just his wife and himself as shareholders, named Nephew Ltd. He paid all the deposits into the company's bank account and it became the share capital as he issued 80,000 ordinary shares, 50,000 to himself and the rest to his wife.'

As we can see from the above, the business was set up on the 1 January 20XX, so we are going to start the cash account on that date with an opening balance of nil.

He then put £80,000 of his own money into the business and issued 80,000 shares to himself and his wife. (A business is always treated as a separate entity to its owners and once formed it becomes a complete entity in its own right.)

As far as the bank account of the business Nephew Ltd is concerned, it started with an opening balance of nil, but it has now received cash in of £80,000 from the issue of shares. So:

Cash Account	
Cash In	£
Issue of Shares	80,000

In addition, the balance sheet will now show £80,000 as shareholders' funds, ie:

Balance Sheet	
Shareholders' Funds	
Ordinary Shares issued – 80,000 @ £1	£80,000

So, the first transaction has effected two of the documents and you can now write the entries described above against the appropriate headings under the cash account and the balance sheet.

Let us look at the next paragraph in the story of John Nephew:

'His first year was very busy and he worked very hard to get the business off to a good start. He was a talented salesman and with invoiced sales at £960,000, against purchases of goods of £720,000, including an accrual he had made for invoices received after the year-end, he was feeling pleased with himself as he came to the end of his first year of trading.'

We will take the items one at a time. First, invoiced sales at £960,000. As we know from the earlier chapters, the profit and loss account is where the results of our trading are shown and thus we enter £960,000 as sales for the year:

Nephew Ltd	
Profit and Loss Account	
For the Year Ending 31 December 20XX	£
Sales	960,000

We also have to make an entry into our cash account as we hope that most of Nephew's customers have paid their invoices. We must, therefore, have received some cash in:

Nephew Ltd
Cash Account
For the Year Ending 31 December 20XX

	£
Opening Balance	nil
Cash In during the year	
Sales	960,000
plus Opening Debtors	
less Closing Debtors	( )

We have used the figures as quoted and have thus not included VAT in these accounts. This is the generally accepted practice as the working of VAT or sales tax is such that the company effectively becomes a tax collector and does not benefit from the money collected, apart from the fact that it sits in the company's bank account for a month or so before being paid over.

The company had collected VAT (sales tax) on its sales and paid VAT on its purchases. All the money collected had been paid over apart from £1,000 that Nephew Ltd had collected in the last quarter but not yet paid. He had been told that his accounts should be presented with all figures shown in the same way as he had described his sales and purchases (ie excluding VAT) and all the figures quoted are exclusive of VAT.

In the books of account the bookkeeper must account correctly for VAT, but the only notice you need to take of VAT on these final documents is to remember to include £1,000 as cash in and also as a current liability, as Nephew Ltd owes the £1,000 that is presently sitting in the company's bank account.

	Cash Account
Cash In	£
VAT (Sales Tax)	1,000
	Balance Sheet
Current Liabilities	£
Non-trade Creditors	1,000

By now you will have got the idea of what you must do to help John Nephew in his predicament and should be feeling reasonably confident that you could have a go at handling the rest of the information.

The task ahead of you is to see if you can complete the cash account, the profit and loss account, the balance sheet, and the cash flow statement from the information given. In addition, you might like to consider whether or not Nephew Ltd had as good a year as John had thought, and ponder on why the bank manager was so worried.

Nephew Ltd – the solution

Always remember in accounting and finance to make the thing as simple as possible. When you are faced with a bewildering mass of detailed transactions, take it easy and take them one at a time. Complete all the book entries on one before moving on to the next. When you have done them all you can then compare your result with the one that follows. Who knows, yours might be better!

Clearly John Nephew needs to set out his company's activities in a way that can give information that can be used to measure performance and reveal strengths and weaknesses. The three accounting documents will all help.

To check our results we will continue through his story: '… against purchases of goods of £720,000, including an accrual that he had made for invoices received after the year-end, he was feeling pleased with himself as he came to the end of his first year of trading.'

When we began to enter the details on the accounts we only dealt with the first half of this paragraph. It is now time to enter the details of Nephew's purchases. The purchases were made as part of Nephew's trading and thus must appear on the profit and loss account as part of the cost of material.

You need to make a note of this cost because we must know the opening and closing stocks before we can work out how many (or rather what value) of those purchases were used in the products that were sold in the year (ie the cost of goods sold). This is described in more detail below, when the closing stock is considered.

Profit and Loss Note	
Purchases	£720,000

If Nephew had all these purchases in the year then it is likely that he paid for some of them, so our cash account needs to show some cash out:

	Cash Out
Purchases	(720,000)
plus Opening Trade Creditors	( )
less Closing Trade Creditors	

The next paragraph in the story as told by John Nephew concerns VAT, which we have dealt with above.

'At the start of the year he had borrowed £100,000 from a bank at an interest of 12 per cent per annum, with the capital sum (£100,000) repayable in equal instalments at the end of each of the next ten years.'

Clearly, then, the company has had cash in of £100,000 on which it has had to pay 12 per cent interest. Thus, the cash account will show:

Cash In	
New Loans	100,000

While the balance sheet as at 1 January 20XX would show:

Long-term Loans	
Bank	100,000

That was the case on 1 January 20XX, but you will have noted that Nephew agreed repayments of the capital sum over ten years in equal amounts. So he must have repaid one tenth of £100,000 at the end of the first year. This also needs to be reflected on the accounts. The company's cash account for the year ended 31 December 20XX would therefore show:

	Cash Out
Bank Loan, Repayment	10,000

And the balance sheet as at 31 December 20XX would now show:

Long-term Loans	
Bank	£90,000

This reflects that a tenth of the loan capital has been repaid (£100,000 – 10,000 = £90,000).

We are still not finished with this item, however, for there are interest payments to be made on the loan.

The repayment of £10,000 was made on the last day of the year and thus the capital sum of £100,000 was present for all but the last day. But, £100,000 @ 12% = £12,000, so £12,000 must have been paid out of cash at bank (or taken by the bank from his account) to cover the interest. This time it will not reduce the capital sum as it was not a repayment. It must, therefore, be a cost that was incurred within the trading of the company and so is charged against the profits on the profit and loss account. The entries are:

Cash Account	
	Cash Out
Interest	£12,000
Profit and Loss Account	
Interest paid	£(12,000)

'He had talked to the bank manager about an overdraft and had an agreement' for ' "the company's day-to-day needs" at an over-draft rate of 18 per cent per annum. Any money on deposit would receive interest at 8 per cent.'

We must wait until we have completed the cash account before we can calculate these interest payments or receipts. In real life, we would calculate them from the daily or monthly cash flow forecast. However, for the purpose of this exercise, and to avoid confusion, it is sufficient to assume that the sum that appears as the closing balance on the cash account has been present all year. It is, therefore, subject to interest at 18 per cent if it is overdrawn, or 8 per cent if it is cash in hand.

'The company had purchased, and paid for, a seven-year lease on business premises for £140,000.'

It seems that he has paid cash out £140,000 from the cash account 'up front' for the lease:

Cash Account	
	Cash Out
Purchase of Lease	£140,000

And, at 1 January, Nephew Ltd had a tangible asset of seven years' occupation of the premises worth £140,000:

Balance Sheet as at 1st January 20XX			
Fixed Assets	cost	depn.	book value
Land & Buildings	140,000	–	£140,000

However, as at 31 December, Nephew Ltd had used up a seventh of that lease, and that use needs to be charged against any profits that were made by using the premises throughout that year.

The asset itself would also have depreciated and as at 31 December 20XX it would only be worth six-sevenths of the original value, ie £140,000 is reduced by the using up of one-seventh of it (£20,000) and the net book value shown on the balance sheet at the end of the year is £120,000. This is entered like so:

Balance Sheet as at 31 December 20XX			
Fixed Assets	cost	depn.	book value
Land & Buildings	140,000	20,000	£120,000

The £20,000 of the lease that was used up in that year would correctly be charged against profits. It would be listed under production costs (if it is the lease of a factory or production unit) and these are generally shown as part of the cost of goods sold. Alternatively, it would appear under expenses (overheads) on the profit and loss account if the lease was for buildings that were not involved in production. (If it's a bit of both then you can get terribly academic and scientifically work out the benefits enjoyed by all the various departments using the buildings and then split the costs in proportion to benefits over all the departments. Or you can do as most accountants do and just choose where you want to show it.) For instance:

Profit and Loss Account

Amortization of Lease   £20,000

He had also bought some plant and equipment for £50,000, which he hoped would last ten years.

Here he has purchased another asset (plant and equipment), so cash out from the cash account must reflect the £50,000 spent on the purchase, and the balance sheet as at 1 January 20XX will show the company owning an asset valued at £50,000.

As with the lease, we would reflect the using up of the asset over its expected lifetime, so we would depreciate the plant and equipment by £5,000. (Here we are using the method of depreciation known as the 'straight-line method', ie £50,000 divided by 10 years = £5,000 per year in depreciation.)

If we put all those entries together they would result in:

Cash Account

                                 Cash Out

Purchase of Plant & Equipment   £50,000

Balance Sheet

Fixed Assets	cost	dprn	book value
Plant & Equipment	50,000	5,000	£45,000

Profit and Loss Account

Depreciation, Plant & Equipment   £5,000

'He bought two second-hand vehicles for the business, which had cost a total of £15,000 and should last him three years, when he would hope to sell them for a total of £3,000.'

This reflects another capital purchase (the purchase of a fixed asset), in this case vehicles. On this capital purchase, however, there is expected to be a residual value (ie the £3,000 the company should get for the vehicles in three years' time).

Depreciation is the attempt to write off the cost of the asset over its lifetime. If we were fairly certain of a residual value then we would deduct that from the cost of the asset and effectively 'write off' (via depreciation) the net cost to the company of £12,000. Thus we would take the £15,000 we have paid out of cash, less the residual value of £3,000 = £12,000, to be depreciated over three years = £4,000 per annum.

If we look at all the transactions that resulted from the above, we would make the following entries in our blank formats of the accounting documents:

Cash Account

	Cash Out
Purchase of Vehicles	£15,000

Balance Sheet

Fixed Assets	cost	dprn	book value
Vehicles	15,000	4,000	£11,000

Profit and Loss Account

Depreciation of Vehicles	£4,000

'At the end of his first year he thought it had been such a good start to the business that he would pay the shareholders (himself and his wife) a dividend of 10 per cent, and was therefore considering the worth of his company…'

It is easy at this point to fall into the trap of thinking of a dividend as being paid out as a percentage of profit, eg a dividend of 10% = 10% of the profits. In fact the percentage quoted is not calculated on profits at all but is a percentage of the issued ordinary share capital.

Thus, in the case of Nephew Ltd, a 10 per cent dividend would be calculated on the issued ordinary shares at nominal value, ie 80,000 shares at a value of £1 each = £80,000 (10% = £8,000).

More care is needed because it states that 'he would pay the shareholders (himself and his wife) a dividend of 10 per cent', not that he *has* paid. So, this amount is still owed by the company to its shareholders and will not appear as cash out. It will instead be listed on the balance sheet among the items we owe.

It would be due to be paid within the following 12 months and so £8,000 would be listed among the current liabilities on the balance sheet. The profit and loss account would show the fact that the directors have proposed to distribute to (pay) the shareholders a sum of £8,000 as dividends, and that amount would be deducted from after-tax profits before calculating the retained profits. It would appear as follows:

Balance Sheet	
Current Liabilities	
Dividends	£8,000
Profit and Loss Account	
Dividends	£8,000

'He looked around the stores and estimated that he had about £48,000 worth of stock at year-end, although a batch that had cost £8,000 was faulty and couldn't be used. Unfortunately he couldn't return it as the supplier had gone bust.'

You will remember that the profit and loss account listed the cost of goods sold, thus:

Profit and Loss Account		
Cost of Goods Sold		
Materials	(	)
Direct Labour	(	)
Factory Expenses	(	)

The materials are calculated by taking the stock we had in the company on the first day of the year (the opening stock) and then adding the value of all the year's materials purchases (this establishes the total value of the stock we had available for sale). We then deduct the stock we were left with at the end of the year (the closing stock). We conclude that the resultant total was the value of the cost of the goods that were sold during the year (and thus include in that figure any stock that went 'walkabout' from the stores).

Nephew's materials charged to the profit and loss account will therefore be:

Profit and Loss Account	
Materials	
Opening stock	nil
Purchases (see earlier)	<u>720,000</u>
	720,000
Closing Stock	<u>(40,000)</u>
Cost of Materials	£680,000
charged to Cost of Goods Sold	

You will see that we have reduced the value of the closing stock by the amount of faulty items that have been found in that closing stock. Clearly we must do this otherwise when we list all we own (on the balance sheet) we will have overstated the value of our closing stock, and accountants have a convention that requires a prudent view to be taken of transactions and asset values.

The profit and loss account would thus appear as above and the balance sheet would contain the entry:

Balance Sheet	
Current Assets	
Stock	£40,000

By reducing the value of the closing stock by any amount, we have effectively increased the cost of goods sold and thus written the items off against profits. No further entries are necessary to cover that item.

If we had left closing stock as £48,000 in the accounts above, our resultant cost of goods sold would have been £720,000 – 48,000 = £672,000. An £8,000 lower charge for cost of goods sold would have resulted in an £8,000 increase in gross profit (sales less cost of sales = gross profit).

We would then have needed to show an entry on the profit and loss account under the heading of obsolete stock for £8,000 to reflect the cost to the company of the useless stock. A similar entry on the balance sheet stock calculation would then be needed to write off the obsolete stock from the value of our assets.

By reducing the closing stock by £8,000 we have reduced the gross profit by £8,000 and, therefore, the trading or operating profit by £8,000, so the faulty stock has been written off. This is the most common way I find it handled in businesses and it is a pity because it disguises just how much obsolescent stock is costing and thus fails to highlight the problem so that a solution can be effected.

'During the year he had employed four people working in production at a total cost of £30,000 and also incurred another £1,610 of production overheads. Fuel and delivery costs were a further £40,000.'

Cash out must account for the actual payment of the wages and fuel and delivery costs that are defined above. These are clearly costs that were incurred in trading so they will appear as charges on the profit and loss account, but where?

The wages are for production staff and are, therefore, clearly a cost of production – they will appear as direct wages under the cost of goods sold.

Production overheads and the fuel and delivery would normally be shown as a cost under the expenses (overheads) section of the profit and loss account. The relevant entries are as follows:

Cash Account

	Cash Out
Production Wages	£30,000
Production Overheads	£1,610
Fuel and Delivery	£40,000

Profit and Loss Account

Cost of Goods Sold	
Direct Wages	£30,000
Overheads	
Production Overheads	£1,610
Fuel and Delivery	£40,000

'Selling and advertising had cost him £56,000, although that sum included a cost (£3,000) for a holiday that he and Mrs Nephew had enjoyed and that had been booked through the company.'

The company is a separate entity to its owners and thus the £3,000 holiday that Mr and Mrs Nephew enjoyed is not a cost of trading. It should, therefore, be charged to their personal accounts or shown as an increased payment to them (with all the income tax implications). We are going to assume that they will repay this sum in the next 12 months, now that they realize the tax implications, and thus show them as a non-trade debtor (someone who owes the company money but not by way of normal trading).

Cash Account	
	Cash Out
Selling and Advertising	£56,000
Profit and Loss Account	
Overheads	
Selling and Advertising	£53,000
Balance Sheet	
Current Assets	
Other Debtors	£3,000

'Administration had cost £8,000 and he paid himself and Mrs Nephew a wage of £1,000 a month each.'

Administration would be listed as an overhead on the profit and loss account and the payment to Mr and Mrs Nephew would be shown in the same section as directors' salaries.

Cash Account	
	Cash Out
Administration	£8,000
Directors' Salaries	£24,000
Profit and Loss Account	
Overheads	
Administration	£8,000
Directors' Salaries	£24,000

'He enjoyed a good relationship with his customers and his terms of trade were for payment in 30 days. In fact, his debtors at the end of his first year on 31 December 20XX were £240,000.'

We now have trade debtors of £240,000 and these are usually shown on the face of the balance sheet listed with all the other debtors under current assets. (You can usually find considerable detail of most items on a balance sheet by referring to the note that is shown against that item. The note against debtors will normally provide the information of the values that have been included under the various types of debtor.)

The debtors of £240,000 is the amount of cash that he has not received from his customers so, in the cash account, we need to deduct the value of his trade debtors from the income shown from sales:

Cash Account		
Opening Balance		nil
Cash In during the year		
Sales		960,000
plus Opening Trade Debtors	nil	
less Closing Trade Debtors	(240,000)	£720,000

'He had settled all the suppliers' invoices he had received by the year-end and all the service invoices. The staff were paid up to date.

'He knew of approximately £60,000 worth of suppliers' invoices that would not be arriving until after the year-end for goods that he had received before the end of the year, most of which were still in stock.'

Nephew's purchases figure includes an accrual to account for the invoices that arrive after the year-end, so it would seem that the total purchases figure is accurate. However, the company did not pay all its suppliers within the year.

The balance sheet as at year-end must therefore show that the company owes £60,000 to its suppliers and this will be shown under current liabilities.

The cash out will also need to reflect the fact that the company did not pay all its suppliers within the year. The entries are made as follows:

Cash Account

	Cash Out
Purchases	(720,000)
plus Opening Trade Creditors	nil
less Closing Trade Creditors	<u>60,000</u>
	(660,000)

Balance Sheet

Current Liabilities	
Trade Creditors	£60,000

Don't forget that we also have a non-trade creditor in the shape of the VATman or VATwoman, to whom we owe £1,000. This will be added to creditors when we put the whole balance sheet together.

'He must pay 42 per cent tax on profits and understood that the capital allowances would work out approximately the same as depreciation, so he could ignore any adjustment of profits and calculate tax on the pre-tax profits shown on a profit and loss account.'

Corporation tax (ie the tax that is paid by companies in the UK) is calculated on the earnings (profits) of the company. We thus need to put together the profit and loss account before we can establish what the tax charge will be.

As we produce the profit and loss account for the year, it is unlikely that we would have paid all our tax liability, but we could have paid some advance corporation tax. To avoid too much complication in this illustration we are going to assume that no advance corporation tax has been paid, and that any tax that is payable as a result of the profits the company made in the year is payable in the following year.

Tax will appear on the profit and loss account as a deduction from pre-tax profits and on the balance sheet as a current liability:

Profit and Loss Account

Taxation	to be calculated when profit is known

Balance Sheet

Current Liabilities	
Taxation	will be owed once profits are known

Details of capital allowances and the tax deductions that can be made when buying or depreciating plant and equipment vary so greatly over the different countries of the world, and at different times within each country, so they are not included in this book. As with all tax matters, they are also subject to constant change, so a visit to a tax accountant is recommended if you have a problem in this area.

Well, I think that's all the transactions complete. How did you get on? A few things should have caused you to ponder, but if you just applied the rules of common sense then you probably completed the task.

Let's now put all of the above together and see what it looks like:

Nephew Ltd		
Profit and Loss Account		
For the year ending 31 December 20XX		
	£	£
Sales		**960,000**
Less Cost of Goods Sold		
Materials	(680,000)	
Direct Labour	(30,000)	
Factory Expenses (deprn)	(5,000)	(715,000)
Gross Profit		**245,000**
Less Overheads (Indirect Expenses)		
Production	(1,610)	
Sales & Marketing	(53,000)	
Delivery (40,000 + deprn 4,000)	(44,000)	
Premises (Lease Amortization)	(20,000)	
Administration (8,000 + 24,000)	(32,000)	(150,610)
Operating (Trading) Profit (PBIT)		94,390
Interest (12,000 + 26,210 on Overdraft)	(38,210)	
Pre-tax Profits		56,180
Taxation (42%)	*(23,590)	
After-tax Profits		32,590
Interim Dividend (paid)	(nil)	
Final Dividend (proposed)	(8,000)	(8,000)
Retained Profits for the Year		24,590
add Retained Profits for Previous Years	(nil)	
Total Retained Profits (Revenue Reserve)	*	£24,590
*Remember to show on the Balance Sheet		

Nephew Ltd
Cash Account
For the Year Ending 31 December 20XX

	£	£
Opening Balance		nil
Cash In during the year		
Sales	960,000	
plus Opening Trade Debtors	nil	
less Closing Trade Debtors	(240,000)	720,000
Issue of Shares	80,000	
New Medium & Long Term Loans	100,000	
Interest Received	–	
Cash from Investments	–	
Disposals of Companies	–	
Cash from other sources	–	180,000
Total Cash Available (Opening Balance + Cash In)		£900,000
Cash Out during the year		
Purchases	(720,000)	
plus Opening Trade Creditors	nil	
less Closing Trade Creditors	60,000	(660,000)
Non-Trade Creditors Increase (Decrease) (VAT)	1,000	
Employee Costs (30,000 + 24,000 Mr & Mrs Nephew)	(54,000)	
Premises Costs (lease)	(140,000)	
Interest Paid on Loan	(12,000)	
Tax Paid (nil, it is assessed this year and payable next)	–	
Dividends Paid (nil as Dividend is only Proposed)	–	
Capital Equipment Purchased (50,000 + 15,000)	(65,000)	
Loan Repayments	(10,000)	
Other Cash Expenditure (40,000 + 1,610 + 53,000 + 3,000 + 8,000)	(105,610)	(385,610)
Sub-total Cash Out		(1,045,610)
Net Cash at Bank or Overdrawn (£900,000 – £1,045,610)		(145,610)

Interest on Overdraft at 18%*   (26,210)
Closing Balance**   £(171,820)

*Remember to charge this additional interest to the profit and loss account
** £171,820 is listed on the balance sheet as the amount we *owe* the bank

---

Nephew Ltd
Balance Sheet as at 31 December 20XX

£	cost	dprn	book value
FIXED ASSETS			
Land & Buildings	140,000	20,000	120,000
Plant & Equipment	50,000	5,000	45,000
Vehicles	15,000	4,000	11,000
	£205,000	£29,000	176,000
		£	£
INVESTMENTS			–
INTANGIBLE ASSETS			–
CURRENT ASSETS			
Stock	40,000		
Debtors (3,000 + 240,000)	243,000		
Cash	nil	283,000	
CURRENT LIABILITIES			
Creditors (£60,000 + VAT)	(61,000)		
Bank Overdraft	(171,820)		
Taxation	(23,590)		
Proposed Dividends	(8,000)	(264,410)	

NET CURRENT ASSETS (£283,000 – £264,410)   18,590

Total Assets less Short-term Liabilities   **194,590**
LONG-TERM LIABILITIES
Loans   90,000

Net ASSET VALUE   **£104,590**

SHAREHOLDERS' FUNDS
Ordinary Shares Issued – 80,000 @ £1   80,000
Preference Shares   nil

Capital Reserve	nil
Revenue Reserve	
(from the P & L Account)	<u>24,590</u>
Total Shareholders' Funds	**£104,590**

Well, how did you do?

The recommended solution given above is no more than that, a recommended solution. Give them to another accountant and he or she may interpret them differently, but they will not change a great deal in substance.

Remember that, whereas bookkeeping is an 'exact' science and all debits must exactly equal the credits, the production of the final accounts (the profit and loss account, the balance sheet and the cash flow statement) is not. Many of the figures are subject to interpretation, but there are always some facts that stand out clearly and cannot be easily disguised (especially when you look at the accounts of a number of years for any one company).

The accountant may carry out certain 'adjustments' that have the effect of improving the profits, or increasing/decreasing the value of the assets shown on the balance sheet but, at the end of the day, there are some fundamentals that do not change.

Accounting 'adjustments' can only be effective over a limited number of years and then the requirements of the double-entry bookkeeping system will make it increasingly impossible to continue to distort the true results. The shrewd reader of audited accounts (published accounts) can usually find the 'adjustments' before the chief executive has 'retired' or moved on to another company.

Now that you have done such a brilliant job on the accounts, we are in a position to examine them to see what they reveal and move you towards the stage where you can confidently discuss the accounts with your accountant.

The first fundamental in Nephew Ltd is that the company must have access to enough cash to pay all its bills, and it is obvious that Nephew Ltd is in serious trouble in this area.

John Nephew negotiated an overdraft of £50,000 to cover the company's day-to-day expenses, but that overdraft has risen to £171,820 by the end of the year. From the tone of the bank manager's letter, it is a situation that has gone beyond his tolerance level.

From the bank manager's point of view, the bank is 'at risk' for £261,820 (the loan, now standing at £90,000, plus the overdraft of £171,820). If things went wrong for the company then the shareholders are 'at risk' (ie how much they stand to lose in the event of the company folding) for the total shareholders' funds of £104,590. The bank is therefore taking a far higher risk than the shareholders, and that is not a situation a bank likes to be in.

What can the bank do about it? A number of things, ranging from taking a charge over the company's assets, through stopping the company's cheques, to putting in the liquidator.

What can John Nephew do to avoid such a catastrophe? What would your advice be? Now that you've completed the accounts, spend a few minutes thinking about the messages they convey. If you really were advising John Nephew, what would you say to him? Take a while looking at the three completed sheets of paper and then write down the main points of advice you would give John Nephew.

Let us suppose that John Nephew looks at all the accounts statements you have produced, and listens to you intently. He then confesses that he is so impressed with the work you have done that he would like you to get even more involved. He offers you some shares in the company. He tells you that he will sell you a further 20,000 shares in Nephew Ltd for the sum of £50,000 (ie £2.50 a share).

Would you scrape up, or borrow, the money and invest in these shares in Nephew Ltd?

Taken aback, you ask a few questions about the company's prospects. John Nephew tells you that he hasn't even begun to penetrate the market yet, and believes he could double the sales from the 100,000 units he sold last year to 200,000 units next year. The existing premises, administration and production overheads could cope with the extra throughput, but the plant and equipment is already at full stretch and he'd need to buy or lease more. He'd also need to double the number of direct workers, and his transport fleet.

He adds that he would need to increase his advertising spend by another £70,000 and take on a first-class salesman at a cost of about £40,000 per annum. Furthermore, next year the company will be paying an interim dividend of 8 per cent and hopes to pay a final dividend of at least 10 per cent.

He believes that, with the £50,000 he will be receiving from you, and with the aid of the accounts you have produced, he will soon be able to convince the bank manager that he's on to a good thing and persuade him to advance the money to cope with the present cash flow problem.

Do you go along with him? Think about it and write down your impressions of the strengths of Nephew Ltd, and the weaknesses. Try to analyse how the company can overcome its pressing cash crisis, or what can be done to appease and satisfy the bank manager.

We look again at Nephew Ltd in the next two chapters, so read on to discover whether your money is safe: have you made a wise investment, or have you lost it all? In the meantime, we are going to produce the cash flow statement for the year ending 31 December 20XX so that you have the three major accounting documents for Nephew Ltd to help your decision making.

Remember that a cash flow statement should reconcile to the differences between the balance sheet at the end of the previous year (ie the opening balance sheet) and the balance sheet at the end of the present year (the closing balance sheet). In the case of Nephew Ltd it was their first year of trading, so the task is made easier by the fact that all the opening balance sheet items are zero.

First, we must discover the net cash inflow or outflow from the company's operations throughout the year. We get the following information from the balance sheet and profit and loss account before moving on to produce the cash flow statement:

Note	This Year
	£
Operating Profit (from P & L Account)	**94,390**
Depreciation (from P & L Account)	9,000
Lease Amortization (from P & L Account)	20,000
(Increase)/Decrease in Stocks (from Balance Sheet)	(40,000)
(Increase)/Decrease in Debtors (from Balance Sheet)	(243,000)
(Decrease)/Increase in Creditors (from Balance Sheet)	61,000
Other non-cash movements	–
Net cash outflow from operating activities	**(98,610)**

Nephew Ltd
Cash Flow Statement

£s	Notes	This Year
Net Cash Outflow from operating	31	**(98,610)**
Net Cash Outflow on investments & servicing of finance		
Interest received		–
Interest paid		(38,210)
Dividends received		–
Dividends paid (nil the dividend is only proposed)		–
Net Cash Outflow on investments and servicing of finance		**(38,210)**
Tax paid		
UK corporation tax paid (nil paid as payment due next year)		–
Net Cash Outflow from investing activities		
Purchase of tangible fixed assets		(205,000)
Purchase of investments		–
Sale of tangible fixed assets		–
Sale of investments		–
Net Cash Outflow from investing activities		**(205,000)**
Net cash (outflow)/inflow before financing		**(341,820)**
Financing		
Issue of ordinary share capital		80,000
New long-term loans		100,000
New short-term loans		–
Repayment of amounts borrowed		(10,000)
Net cash (outflow)/inflow from financing		**170,000**
(Decrease)/increase in cash & equivalent		**(171,820)**
add Net cash at beginning of the year		–
Net cash (overdraft) at end of the year		**(171,820)**

An overdraft of £(171,820) reconciles with the figure shown on the Balance Sheet.

In this chapter we have looked at the effect of each individual transaction on the cash account, the profit and loss account and the balance sheet. We have then produced a cash flow statement that reconciles to the other three documents and summarizes the company's use of cash. I tried to encourage you to have a go at completing the documents on your own and if you did then it would be interesting to turn back the pages at this point to see how well you did.

One of the great problems of finance and accounting is that the slightest mistake can throw out the balances and thus cause huge problems when you come to reconcile the accounts. Examiners love to test students on all the types of errors that can cause the trial balance not to balance, but that is not the purpose of this book – I leave that to the teachers of bookkeeping. This book is aimed at the non-accountant and the student who wish to gain a better understanding of finance so that they can communicate with their accountants and feel more confident when dealing with their company's management accounts and published accounts.

The dialogue that runs through the book tries to shed some light on how accounts are actually used, rather than concentrate on the theoretical perfect production of the figures. It thus aims to give you the reader a practical knowledge of how the accounting documents can be of help to you in your daily occupation.

If you have reached this far and been able to follow my descriptions in the solution to Nephew Ltd then you have already accomplished a great deal. The key is being able to follow the solution rather than being able to complete the books of account; we have accountants to do that for you. If you are at this stage then we can begin to use the documents to measure past performance and also to project forward into the future. We might even be able to indicate where strengths and weaknesses exist within a company or an organization. The next two chapters will be of great interest to you.

8

Forecasting and budgeting

In Chapter 7 we built a cash account, a profit and loss account, a balance sheet and a cash flow statement for Nephew Ltd for all the transactions that took place in the year-ending 31 December 20XX and we were left with a few conundrums:

1. How can John Nephew prevent the bank from taking drastic action against the company?
2. How can Nephew Ltd improve its cash flow?
3. Should you buy the 20,000 newly issued shares for £50,000?
4. What would be the result if John were able to 'double the sale next year' under the conditions he described?

To answer these questions we must first examine the accounts that appeared towards the end of Chapter 7, and now is a good time for you to remind yourself of the main features of Nephew Ltd's 20XX accounts.

Nephew Ltd's bank manager had agreed an overdraft at 18 per cent to cover the 'day-to-day needs' of the company. Defining day-to-day needs is always a nebulous task but £171,820 overdrawn against an agreed limit of £50,000 in a company where the bank has already given a loan (now standing at £90,000, making total borrowings equal to £261,820), and where the total shareholders' equity (total shareholders' funds) only amounts to £104,590, is not guaranteed to make your bank manager sleep easily at night.

One way of improving his or her peace of mind may be to offer the bank a charge over the assets of the company (although it is inconceivable that they would have granted you the loan and overdraft without security, even if you do play golf with your bank manager). A charge over the assets is similar to the way a mortgage company takes a charge over your house. If you fail to pay the monies due on your mortgage then they can seize the house from you and sell it to recover all you owe them. (In theory, if they sell the house for more than you owe them they should pay the surplus funds back to you, but it is surprising how seldom that occurs.)

A charge over the assets shouldn't be easily given away as you begin to lose some control over your ability to manage them and you are always at risk of the bank deciding to call in its overdraft (ie telling you that you cannot issue any more cheques until the overdraft is nil). In such a situation you usually lose everything including the ability to continue trading. In the case of Nephew Ltd it seems to have little choice but to offer the bank some such security.

How can John Nephew prevent the bank from taking drastic action against the company?

It would seem that he must offer them the security of a charge over the assets. That would help, but he must also reassure the bank manager that he is going to get his cash flow under control in the immediate future.

A charge over the assets will not answer all the company's cash problems. The bank is aware that in a break-up situation you hardly ever get the full book value for a company's assets, and it would probably reduce the value shown on the balance sheet by 50 per cent when holding them as a security.

You will see from the balance sheet that the total asset value equals £459,000 (£176,000 of fixed assets, plus £283,000 of current assets).

Fifty per cent of £459,000 equals £229,500, so the total indebtedness to the bank (£261,820) is only just covered and almost certainly rated as poorly secured in the bank manager's eyes, even if the charge included all the assets of the company rather than just the fixed assets. However, you can remind him that the year to 31 December 20XX was a start-up year and, as such, was very expensive on cash. Maybe next year will be better, but then again maybe it will not! It is the 'maybes' of this world that banks and financiers don't like.

If you have a plan, it should be possible to put it down on paper and work out the expected financial returns before committing to it. Had John Nephew done that in advance of 20XX then he could have planned the company's cash flow in a way that would have prevented the situation he is now in – a situation, furthermore, that could turn 'fatal' at any moment.

If he had known in advance that the bank might panic just at the moment when he was celebrating the success of the company, he could have made other arrangements. For example, it might have been possible to have taken a lease with an annual payment instead of £140,000 up-front. This might have proved more expensive, but it can be seen from the profit and loss account that the company could afford to pay a little more and still make profits. What it cannot afford is £140,000 cash up-front, not with all the other up-front money that was required. Payments spread over the seven years of the lease would have allowed the company to generate the required cash from its operations over that time.

It might also have been possible to lease the plant and equipment instead of purchasing it outright. Again, this might have proved to be a little more expensive but it would have spread the cash over the life of the asset instead of requiring it all at the front-end.

Those two arrangements alone would have preserved cash resources in the company amounting to £160,000 in the critical first year.

Another look at the balance sheet reveals that the company's trade debtors (its customers) owe £240,000. According to the profit and loss account, the sales were £960,000. If we divide that by 12 then the company is averaging sales of £80,000 a month.

The debtor figure of £240,000 thus represents three months (90 days) of sales (ie $3 \times £80,000 = £240,000$. If you wish to calculate it another way, it took 365 days to sell £960,000 of sales; £240,000 is one quarter of £960,000; one quarter of a year is three months = 90 days.) Its customers are therefore taking, on average, 90 days to pay their invoices although the terms of trade (Chapter 7) are 30 days.

If the company could succeed in chasing earlier payment from its customers, it might cure the cash flow crisis that the company is now facing. If customers were to pay on time (30 days) then Nephew Ltd's bank account would receive the sum of £160,000 (ie instead of the money being in the customers' banks it would have been paid into Nephew Ltd's bank account).

It is not easy to get customers to pay on time and many companies are notoriously bad about even trying. If you put your mind to it then it is possible, and even if the company were only to reduce it to 45 days then it would still bring in cash of £120,000 (£240,000 is 90 days so divide by 2).

Another source of cash is the trade creditors (the company's suppliers). As discussed above, the company's customers (debtors) are taking 90 days to pay their bills while Nephew Ltd is paying its suppliers in 32 days.

It can be seen from the profit and loss account (page 146) that in the year 20XX Nephew Ltd made £680,000 worth of purchases of materials and the balance sheet (page 148) reveals that its trade creditors at year-end were £60,000. (60/680 as a proportion of the year of 365 days works out at 32.2 days.) The full definitions of debtor and creditor days, and how to calculate them, are given in the next chapter.

At worst, you should be taking as long to pay your suppliers as your customers are taking to pay you. If you increased your creditors to the same 45 days that you are attempting to get your debtors to pay in then you hold on to your money for 12.8 days longer before sending it to your suppliers. (£680,000/365 = £1,863 average purchases in a day times 12.8 = £23,847 in 12 days.)

It may be that the stock situation could also be improved. The company is sitting on 20 days of stock, ie the balance sheet reveals a closing stock value of £40,000. This is usually valued at the cost of materials plus the labour that has worked on it plus any factory overheads. The profit and loss reveals that a total of £715,000 was spent in the year on these items. Thus, £40,000 as a proportion of £715,000 times 365 days of a year equates to 20.4 days.

The type of trade and the length of the production and delivery cycles define the number of days of stock that is necessary to successfully support a business. However, it is true to say that there are very few businesses that cannot get their stock days down to single figures if they really wanted to. If you halve the amount of stock lying around in the company, you inject another

£20,000 into the company's bank account. The cash management of the company is, therefore, a disaster.

The company takes 20 days to turn its stock around (ie 20 days from the time of receipt to the time it has been manufactured into a finished product and then sold). It pays the supplier 12 days later, but after paying the supplier from cash it has had to borrow from the bank. It then waits another 78 days to get its money in from its customers. No wonder the overdraft has shot up so high, particularly when some of the long-term capital (fixed assets) has been financed with short-term borrowings.

How desperate is the situation? Well, the shareholders, who provided capital of £80,000, and the ten-year loan of £100,000, are presumably locked into the company for some years ahead and not likely to be withdrawn if the bank manager suddenly feels insecure, whereas the overdraft could be withdrawn tomorrow.

The company has purchased £205,000 worth of fixed assets, so at least £25,000 (£180,00 came from long-term borrowings and shareholders' funds) worth of the overdraft has gone to funding the long-term assets. The way the company is being run at present, another £190,410 (£283,000 less the £92,590 owed to creditors, tax and in dividends) is needed to fund the short-term assets.

How can Nephew Ltd improve its cash flow?

As we discussed above, if it was possible to renegotiate the lease to annual payments then this would produce cash of £120,000 on an immediate basis and this, along with the other improvements we discussed, would bring in:

Lease renegotiated	£120,000
Debtor days to 45	£120,000
Creditor days to 45	£22,500
Stock days to 10	£20,000
Cash in resulting from these management actions	**£282,500**

So maybe the cure was in John Nephew's hands all the time.

You would be surprised by how often the situation illustrated by the story of Nephew Ltd is repeated in real life in companies large and small throughout the UK, Europe, the USA and most other areas of the world. A great deal of my consultancy work is refocusing management to the financial facts of life, and Nephew Ltd is a perfect illustration of the returns that are possible for such work. (If you add three noughts to the above figures then you are dealing in the amounts of cash that can be recovered from many a public limited company.)

If John Nephew had not called for help when he did, then a potentially highly successful company would have gone 'down the tubes' as the liquidators moved in.

So, you have helped John Nephew identify a way of improving the company's weakest area, its cash flow. OK so far, but should you buy the 20,000 newly issued shares he's offered you for £50,000? There are a few things you should bear in mind.

In 20XX, the after-tax profits (the profits that are left for the shareholders after all other costs are allowed for – often called the earnings of the company) was £32,590 (page 146). There were 80,000 shares issued, so the *earnings per share* was 41p (£32,590 divided by 80,000).

As the shares had cost John Nephew and his wife £1 each, he therefore received an excellent return on his first year. Indeed, at that rate of return, they would get their money back in just under three years (2.7 years in fact).

The price paid for the share divided by the earnings per share is called the p/e ratio and equals 2.45 (£1.00 divided by 41p = 2.45).

However, if you buy an additional 20,000 shares, there will be 100,000 ordinary shares issued. Your £50,000 will improve the company's cash flow, but if it is just used for that, rather than to increase profitability, and there is no profit improvement, then after-tax profits of £32,590 must cover 100,000 shares. Next year's earnings per share would fall to approximately 33p (32.6p to be exact).

You will have paid £2.50 a share (£50,000 for 20,000 shares) and the p/e therefore becomes 250/32.6 = 7.7.

If you look at the share prices in the morning newspapers, or on Ceefax or the Internet, you will often see the p/e quoted. You can look up the variations and approximate average for the type of company you are following (ie most newspapers list the quoted companies according to their trade sector and it is easier to see an average for that trade sector). We will assume that a p/e of 7.7 is somewhere near the mark at which shares trade on the stock exchange for this type of company.

It would seem, therefore, that the price of £2.50 a share asked by John Nephew is not unreasonable based on past performance (be it for only one year) and you are now left with two major dilemmas:

One – If you pay over £50,000 to the company, what is to stop the bank from pulling the rug out and putting the liquidators in, resulting in you losing all your money?

Two – What will be the result, at the end of next year, of John Nephew's ambitious plans for the company?

Should you buy the 20,000 newly issued shares for £50,000?

The price is not unreasonable, but you would probably need to insist that the management of the company pay greater attention to cash management, and that preventing the bank from taking drastic action while improving cash flow must be the company's first priority.

You would also need to evaluate John Nephew's plans for the company throughout the following year before committing yourself. It would be a tragedy if your excellent advice pulled the company out of the hole it is now in, only for it to fall immediately down another as it presses ahead with the expansion.

You need to consider precisely the effects on the company if John was able to 'double the sales next year'.

At the end of Chapter 7, we heard that: 'he hasn't even begun to penetrate the market yet, and believes he could double the sales from the 100,000 units he sold in 20XX to 200,000 units next year'. He went on to say that 'the existing premises, administration and production overheads could cope with the extra throughput, but the plant and equipment is already at full stretch and he'd need to buy or lease more.'

He'd also 'need to double the number of workers, and his transport fleet'. He told you that he 'would need to increase his advertising spend by another £70,000 and take on a first-class salesman at a cost of about £40,000 per annum'. He adds that 'next year the company will be paying an interim dividend of 8 per cent and hopes to pay a final dividend of at least 10 per cent.'

At this point, you can either produce an 'extract' of the profit and loss account, balance sheet and the cash account, or the cash

flow statement, for the year ahead, or produce the reports in full
for your estimate of next year's performance of Nephew Ltd. If
you produce a forecast for next year you can then make comparisons with the year just past and see the effect of any proposals
the company has for improved performance. The £50,000 you
might be willing to drum up to invest in the company is dependent upon future performance, not past.

You have already established that the previous way of
managing cash was a disaster that almost closed the company, so
we are going to assume that John Nephew has accepted the
wisdom of your ultimatum that the company must reduce debtor
(customer) days and increase creditor (supplier) days to 45. He
has also set in motion a stock-reduction programme and hopes to
have his stocks down to ten days by the end of the year.

John Nephew tells you that the company was unable to do
anything about the lease, but was able to sell and lease back its
plant and equipment. It received the sum of £30,000. Now that it
no longer owns the asset, the company must pay the finance
house, which arranged the deal, the sum of £13,000 a year for the
old equipment and a further £13,000 for the new equipment for
the next three years, and a peppercorn thereafter.

The bank has agreed to support the company for one more year
at a maximum overdraft of £100,000; its lending has now been
secured by a charge over the assets of the company. The bank
manager insists that the rate of interest on the overdraft must
remain at 18 per cent, and he will pay only 8 per cent on any
money that is in the account.

What would be the result if John were able to 'double the sales next year'?

We can find this out by running the changes through the accounts
documents to produce a forecast of the next year's set of
accounts. This is a task you can do without any assistance, and in
so doing you will consolidate all the knowledge you have gained
from this book so far.

First, a few things to bear in mind:

- If sales double, then the cost of the materials used to make the
  goods (the materials costs shown in the cost of goods sold)
  will be expected to double.

- If sales double then the 45 days of debtors you are insisting upon will be 45 days of next year's level of sales (45/365 times next year's sales).
- If the sales double and thus the materials double then the purchases (subject to any adjustments in stock) and creditors will be 45 days of next year's purchases
- If sales throughput doubles and stock stays at £40,000 then the stock will be ten days of next year's cost of goods sold
- For next year, the company now has: opening debtors (= the closing debtors on the 20XX accounts); opening creditors (=closing creditors on the 20XX accounts); opening stock (= closing stock on the 20XX accounts).
- In addition, the company also has an opening cash balance (£171,820 overdraft) with which it finished the year 20XX.

All the improvements in cash management you demanded will come into effect during next year, but cannot now change the 20XX figures as that year has passed.

We can assume that the amount held in VAT will double next year due to the doubling of the throughput.

Why don't you try out your newly acquired skills and produce the forecasts for next year? You are producing precisely the same accounts as we have used in the earlier chapters except that you are now heading them as follows:

Nephew Ltd		
CASH ACCOUNT	ACTUAL	FORECAST
For the Years Ended 31 December	20XX	20X1

You might also find it easier to work in thousands of pounds or, better still, to one decimal place of a thousand pounds. For example:

Nephew Ltd		
CASH ACCOUNT	ACTUAL	FORECAST
For the Years Ended 31 December	20XX	20X1
Opening Balance	nil	(171.8)
CASH IN		
Sales	960.0	1,920.0
plus Opening Debtors	nil	240.0
less Closing Debtors	(240.0)	(236.7)*
Cash In from Sales	720.0	1,923.3

*You have insisted upon improved cash management and this included controlling the company's credit customers to an average of 45 days. Sales for 20X1 are expected to double to £1,920,000, divided by 365 = 1 day average sales, then times 45 = £236,712 as the value of the 45 days of debtors at the end of the year.

It is said that we retain about 10–15 per cent of what we hear, about 20–30 per cent of what we see and about 40–50 per cent of what we do.

We all live very busy lives these days, but if you make the time to construct your own forecast of the financial results of Nephew Ltd for next year before you check them out with the solution that follows then you will maximize the learning you can get from this book.

There are some tricky points and these are explained in the notes that end this chapter, but try it for yourself and see how much you can get right without looking at the solution. The principle behind every point has been explained in earlier pages. If you don't manage to get any figures in the correct place then it will have established which parts of the book you need to go over again.

Have a go, there's nothing to lose.

Nephew Ltd

CASH ACCOUNT	ACTUAL	FORECAST
£000s – for the Years Ending 31 December	20XX	20X1
Opening Balance	**nil**	**(171.8)**
CASH IN		
Sales	960.0	1,920.0
plus Opening Debtors	nil	240.0
less Closing Debtors	(240.0)	(236.7)
	720.0	1,923.3
Sale of Fixed Assets		30.0
Issue of Shares	80.0	50.0
New Medium & Long-term Loans	100.0	–
Interest Received	–	–
Cash from other sources	–	–
Total Cash Available (Opening Balance + Cash In)	**£900.0**	**£1,831.5**
CASH OUT		
Purchases (Materials used – O. Stock + C. Stock)	(720.0)	(1,360.0)
plus Opening Trade Creditors	–	(60.0)
less Closing Trade Creditors	60.0	167.7
	(660.0)	(1,252.3)
Non-trade Creditors Increase (Decrease) (VAT)	1.0	1.0
Employee Costs (labour + directors + holiday)	(57.0)	(87.0)
Premises Costs	(140.0)	–
Tax Paid	–	(23.6)
Dividends Paid (last year + this year's interim)	–	(16.0)
Capital Equipment Purchased (vehicles)	(65.0)	(15.0)
Capital Equipment Leased (P & E)	–	(26.0)
Loan Repayments	(10.0)	(10.0)
New Advertising	–	(70.0)
Other Cash Expenditure – sales and marketing	(53.0)	(93.0)
transport	(40.0)	(80.0)
production	(1.6)	(1.6)
administration	(8.0)	(8.0)

*Interest Paid on Loan	(12.0)	(10.8)*
Sub-total Cash Out	**1,045.6**	**1,692.3**
Net Cash at Bank or Overdrawn	(145.6)	139.2
* Interest on Overdraft at 18		
(8% on deposits)	(26.2)	11.1*
Closing Balance	**£(171.8)**	**£150.3**

Nephew Ltd
Profit and Loss Account

For the Years Ending 31 December	20XX	20X1
£000s	Actual	Forecast
Sales	960.0	1,920.0
Less COST OF GOODS SOLD		
Materials	(680.0)	(1,360.0)
Direct Labour	(30.0)	(60.0)
Factory Expenses (P&E lease)	(5.0)	(26.0)
	(715.0)	(1,446.0)
GROSS PROFIT	**245.0**	**474.0**
Less OVERHEADS (Indirect Expenses)		
Production	(1.6)	(1.6)
Sales & Marketing (+ advert		
+ new salesman)	(53.0)	(163.0)
Delivery (incl. depn)	(44.0)	(88.0)
Premises (Lease Amortization)	(20.0)	(20.0)
Administration (£8.0 + £24.0)	(32.0)	(32.0)
Loss on Sale of Asset	–	(15.0)
	(150.6)	(319.6)
OPERATING (TRADING) **PROFIT** (PBIT)	**94.4**	**154.4**
Interest (Loan + Overdraft,		
see Cash Account)	(38.2)	0.3
PRE-TAX PROFITS	**56.2**	**154.7**
Taxation (42%)	(23.6)	(65.0)
After-tax Profits	32.6	89.7
Interim Dividend (paid)	–	(8.0)
Final Dividend (proposed)	(8.0)	(10.0)
	(8.0)	(18.0)

RETAINED PROFITS for the Year	24.6	71.7
add Retained Profits for Previous Years	–	24.6
Total Retained Profits	£24.6	£96.3

Nephew Ltd

Balance Sheet as at 31 December	20XX	20X1
£000s	Actual	Forecast
FIXED ASSETS		
Land & Buildings	120.0	100.0
Plant & Equipment	45.0	–
Vehicles	11.0	18.0
	176.0	118.0
INVESTMENTS	–	–
INTANGIBLE ASSETS	–	–
CURRENT ASSETS		
Stock	40.0	40.0
Debtors (inc. Mr & Mrs Nephew's holiday)	243.0	242.7
Cash	–	150.3
Total Current Assets	283.0	433.0
CURRENT LIABILITIES		
Creditors (including VAT)	(61.0)	(169.7)
Bank Overdraft	(171.8)	–
Taxation	(23.6)	(65.0)
Dividends	(8.0)	(10.0)
Total Current Liabilities	(264.4)	(244.7)
NET CURRENT ASSETS (CA – CL)	18.6	188.3
Total assets less short-term liabilities	194.6	306.3
LONG-TERM LIABILITIES		
Loans	(90.0)	(80.0)
Net ASSET VALUE	£104.6	£226.3
SHAREHOLDERS' FUNDS		
Ordinary Shares £1 Issued	80.0	100.0
Preference Shares	–	–
Capital Reserve	–	30.0

	24.6	96.3
Revenue Reserve	24.6	96.3
TOTAL Shareholders' Funds	**£104.6**	**£226.3**

Nephew Ltd
Cash Flow Statement for the year ending 20X1

£000s	20XX Actual	20X1 Forecast
Net cash outflow from operating	**(98.6)**	306.4
Net cash outflow on investments an servicing of finance		
Interest received	–	11.1
Interest paid	(38.2)	(10.8)
Dividends received	–	–
Dividends paid (last year's final + this year's interim)	–	(16.0)
	(38.2)	**(15.7)**
Tax paid		
UK corporation tax paid (last year's tax)	–	**(23.6)**
Net cash outflow from investing activities		
Purchase of tangible fixed assets (vehicle)	(205.0)	(15.0)
Purchase of investments	–	
Sale of tangible fixed assets (p & e)	–	30.0
Net cash outflow from investing activities	**(205.0)**	**15.0**
Net cash (outflow)/inflow before financing	**(341.8)**	**282.1**
Financing		
Issue of ordinary share capital	80.0	50.0
New long-term loans	100.0	–
Loan repayment	(10.0)	(10.0)
Net cash (outflow)/inflow from financing	**170.0**	**40.0**
(Decrease)/increase in cash and equivalent	**(171.8)**	**322.1**
add Net cash at beginning of the year	–	(171.8)
Net cash (overdraft) at end of the year	**£(171.8)**	**£150.3**

Note	20XX	20X1
Operating profit	94.4	154.4
Depreciation	9.0	8.0
Lease amortization	20.0	20.0
(Increase)/decrease in stocks	(40.0)	–
(Increase)/decrease in debtors	(243.0)	0.3
(Decrease)/increase in creditors	61.0	108.7
Other non-cash movements	–	15.0
Net cash outflow from operating activities	**£(98.6)**	**£306.4**

Well, how did you do? Remember that final accounts are really the accountant's interpretation of the facts and events that the company has been through (or, in the case of a forecast, will go through) in the time-scale defined in the title. So, it could be that your interpretation is better than mine. However, for the moment we are going to concentrate on the set of accounts that has been produced on the previous few pages. Please take time to study them before we proceed with the analysis of the forecast.

We will make the assumption that it is now 1 January 20X1, so we can do nothing about the 20XX results except to learn from them, and to use them for comparisons. We will therefore concentrate our attentions for management action upon the 20X1 forecast.

The first thing to realize about any forecast is that it is guesswork. None of us can see the future clearly (otherwise we'd all be millionaires). We are only human, and as such we must make the best guess as to what is going to happen in the future.

Often the more skilful the manager, the more accurate are his guesses, but this is not always so. The real fascination of management is that there can be as many ideas of what the future holds as there are managers. In fact, in a healthy company that is precisely the case. At the end of the day the board of directors have to take the distilled wisdom of all the various ideas and decide which they are 'going to run with', ie to which are they going to commit the company's (and therefore the shareholders') money.

In the case of Nephew Ltd, we are confining our thoughts to the strong and weak points, assuming that John Nephew can actually double sales in the year as he promised. (In real life we would do a sensitivity analysis on the plans to get a better feeling of the accuracy and risks.)

The first point of satisfaction must be the results of imposing some cash management on the company. No longer is the company acting as unpaid, interest-free bankers to its customers. Debtors and creditors are now both at a reasonably respectable 45 days, with stock reduced to ten days.

As a result of these improvements in the control of working capital, plus the sale and lease-back of the plant and equipment and the leasing of new equipment, the company no longer has an overdraft at a level that was threatening to cripple or liquidate it. It is now expected to have funds (£150,300) in the bank on deposit by the end of 20X1. (This might equally be thought of as unsound management, as we shall see in Chapter 9.)

You might care to work out the effect on the company's plans had you not imposed the discipline of cash management. If Nephew Ltd had doubled the sales without improving their cash management, with 90 days of trade debtors (the level they had at the end of 20XX), then the company would have been forced to use up cash resources by leaving their money in their customers' bank accounts instead of getting it into their own. This sum would have amounted to £473,425 (90/365 x £1,920,000) instead of the £236,700 needed under your plan. A difference of £236,725 of additional cash would have been needed.

Good cash management has enabled the company to hold on to £167,700 of suppliers' money by buying on 45 days of credit. If they had continued paying at 32 days then they would have owed their trade creditors £119,233 (£1360/365 x 32). A difference of £48,467 of additional cash would have been needed.

The company would also have needed £80,000 for stock if it continued to operate at 20 days instead of the ten days you have demanded. A difference of £40,000 of additional cash would have been needed.

So, by sound management of non-working capital throughout 20X1 the company has saved £325,192 and thus has cash in the bank to use on other projects or ventures (always assuming that it can manage them).

You will remember that the bank manager restricted the overdraft to £100,000 throughout 20X1. Had the cash management at Nephew Ltd remained as lax in 20X1 as it had been in 20XX, the bank balance would not have been £150,300 in funds, but

£174,892 overdrawn (£150,300 less the above adjustment of £325,192), and well above the agreed limit.

The overdraft would have been increased further by the purchase of the new equipment that has now been leased. There are many bank managers who would refuse to honour cheques in situations that are much better than that. So if you didn't manage to convince John Nephew of the wisdom of sound cash management maybe you'd lose all your money after all.

If you really have convinced John Nephew of the virtues of sound monetary and cash management then who knows, you may be sitting on a fortune, such is the fine line that often separates success from failure.

From the shareholders' point of view, if the company can achieve the 20X1 forecast then it will enjoy earnings per share of 89.7p (after-tax profits of £89,700 divided by the 100,000 ordinary shares issued). With such a high eps (earnings per share) you would expect the share price to go soaring up in the market place.

If Nephew Ltd was a publicly quoted company and we can assume, as we did earlier, that a p/e (price/earnings) of about 7.7 was about right for this type of company, then the market price for Nephew Ltd at the end of 20X1 (assuming it can achieve its forecast) would probably be around 690 (£6.90 per share) or higher. This was arrived at by the fact that £6.90 is 7.7 times the eps of 89.7p (thus 690 divided by eps of 89.7 gives a p/e of 7.7).

It would seem, therefore, that if John Nephew has learnt the virtues of sound cash management, and his judgement and forecasting can be trusted and is accurate, then your investment of £50,000 for 20,000 ordinary shares may be the best you ever made. You bought the shares for £2.50 each (£50,000 divided by 20,000) and by the end of 20X1 they are expected to be trading at £6.90 a share. This would value your holding of shares at a splendid £138,000 (20,000 shares times the £6.90 they are trading at). Not bad for a single year's return!

The stock market invests in the future expectations of profits rather than past performance. It is future profits that earn the shareholder money (either by way of dividends or on the increase in the share price enabling the owner to sell his shares at a profit). If it seemed that such an increase in the after-tax profits of the company were likely to continue into the following years then there would be considerable demand for the shares of

Nephew Ltd, and more people wanting to buy rather than sell will bid the price up.

A high p/e can therefore be a sign that the stock market is expecting better results (after-tax profits) in the future than it had last year. A low p/e indicates the reverse and that people are trying to get out of your share before the price and the profits drop too low. It could also, of course, be the result of rumoured takeover activities involving other companies, or the company itself.

All this dealing in shares affects the company in that the board of directors runs the company on behalf of the shareholders. (This may come as news to some directors.) Shareholders are not going to be very happy if the price of the shares on the stock market begins to fall, and they get particularly upset when it drops below the price they paid for them.

None of this dealing appears in the accounts of the company. Once the company has issued a share then it is entered in the accounts as ordinary shares issued at the nominal value of the share (eg £1 a share if they are £1 shares). Any money received by the company for that share that is over and above the nominal (or par) value is shown in the share premium account (which is normally listed among the capital reserves).

For example:

The company issues 20,000 ordinary shares with a par (nominal) value of £1 and receives £50,000 for them.

The cash account receives the £50,000 as cash in.

The ordinary shares account shows an increase of 20,000 shares issued at £1 = £20,000.

The share premium account shows an increase of £30,000, being 20,000 times the premium that was paid on each share (ie price paid = £2.50, but the nominal value = £1, thus premium = £1.50 per share).

Once the share is issued then the owner of a share in a publicly quoted company may trade the share with pretty well whoever he pleases, and he (not the company) receives the money from such a sale.

The stock market fluctuates constantly as supply and demand as well as external factors affect the price of every share, so the market price of the share is seldom disclosed in the accounts.

So if we've established that Nephew Ltd operated sound cash management, and you had confidence in John Nephew, then you could make a lot of money over the next 12 months.

Could this be so in real life? The answer has to be yes, but you are unlikely to be able to assert as much influence on most boards of directors as you were with John Nephew, and the opportunity to double turnover doesn't come to every company. Having said that, however, there are a remarkable number of companies that could substantially improve performance, and maybe even double turnover, if only their executive managers had the knowledge, and the cash, to finance their key managers' ideas.

Sadly, all too often, all the cash they need is tied up in the company without their knowledge, and they go on spending 60 to 70 hours a week pursuing the 'bottom line' on borrowed cash.

There are many lessons in Nephew Ltd for a lot of companies in real life, big and small. For many of them it would be a disaster if they went ahead with many of their plans without first getting their cash management house in order. There is often enough cash tied up in the traditional company to do nearly everything it wanted, including the leap into quantum profits, if only it knew how to tap that resource.

In the next chapter we look at a number of factors and ratios that will help you put your finger on the strengths and weaknesses of even the most complex company.

Take care, though: 20X1 is only a forecast.

Notes to the 20X1 forecast

Cash account

The opening balance on the 20X1 cash account is the balance we had at the bank at the end of the previous year, ie the £171.8 (thousand) overdraft.

Sales have been taken at John Nephew's forecast, ie twice the 20XX level.

The opening debtors, creditors and stock are the balances we were left with at the end of the previous year.

Closing debtors are equivalent to 45 days of 20X1 sales and closing debtors 45 days of 20X1 Purchases. Closing stock is taken at the same level as in 20XX.

If sales have doubled then the materials used in the goods that were sold must have doubled, and materials listed in the cost of goods sold is twice the 20XX figure.

Purchases represent the purchase of the materials (and services where appropriate) and this would usually be the cost of materials as adjusted by stocks. In this instance the opening and closing stock remain at the same level, ie £40,000, so the company had to purchase the £1,360,000 worth of materials it needed to make the goods it sold in 201X:

Materials		
Opening Stock	40	
Purchases	1,360	1,400
Less Closing Stock		40
Materials needed to be purchased in year		£1,360

In the cash account, the plant and equipment purchased in 20XX was sold and leased back in 20X1. The sale for £30,000 is represented in the cash in while the lease costs are included under cash out as capital equipment leased.

The company received £50,000 cash in from the issue of new shares to you.

It never received the £3,000 non-trade debtor that was owed by Mr and Mrs Nephew for their holiday and, at the end of the year 20X1, it is assumed that they booked another holiday valued at £3,000, which they put 'through the books'. These amounts account for the difference between the trade debtors and the total debtors shown on the balance sheet

The additional £1,000 cash for a non-trade creditor that it had collected on the sales tax (VAT) was included in creditors on the balance sheet and represents the difference in value from the trade creditors.

The loan is repaid at the end of each year so the balance on the loan account would have been £90,000 all year apart from the last day. Interest paid at 12 per cent on £90,000 = £10,800.

The tax paid is the amount that was shown on the 20XX balance sheet under current liabilities as owed. The dividends paid in 20X1 was the final dividends of 20XX that was shown on the balance sheet as outstanding, plus the interim dividend of

20X1 (which is usually paid in the latter half of the financial year, ie July–Dec 20X1).

John Nephew indicated that the cost of fuel and delivery would double. Though it might have been possible to get the second-hand vehicles bought in 20XX to do double the amount of work, it seemed prudent, in the absence of any other information, to allow for the company buying more vehicles on the same terms as in 20XX.

On the last day of the year, the bank is expecting the repayment of another £10,000 of the loan.

When calculating the interest payment, the cash account we have drawn up makes the assumption that the cash balance, or overdraft, was present all year, though this would clearly not be the case. In real life, if a forecast such as the above looked as though it might be feasible then a detailed cash flow forecast (Chapter 5) would be necessary on, at longest, a month-by-month basis. This would identify potential cash problems throughout the set-up time for the project and also enable you to work out the cash balance or overdraft, and the interest thereon, with a great deal more accuracy (subject to the inaccuracies inherent in forecasting).

Profit and loss account

Many of the items that appear on the profit and loss account have been described under the cash account. We define below those that have changed and have not already been explained, or those that might need a little extra explanation.

The £26,000 of factory expenses consist of the lease of £13,000 on the old equipment that had been sold and leased back and £13,000 p.a. on the new equipment.

Sales and marketing has been increased by the salary of the new salesman (£40,000) plus the advertising campaign (£70,000).

Delivery is doubled in line with John Nephew's statement and the doubling of the vehicle fleet described under the cash account.

The plant and equipment was 'in the books' at £45,000, ie at the end of the previous year the balance sheet showed:

> ## Nephew Ltd
> ### Balance Sheet as at 31 December 20XX
>
> | Fixed Assets | cost | dprn | book value |
> |---|---|---|---|
> | Plant & Equipment | 50,000 | 5,000 | £45,000 |

Thus the asset (plant and equipment) stood in the books at a value of £45,000. On the sale and leaseback deal it was sold for £30,000. Therefore, the company made a loss on the sale of the asset of £15,000. (Can I hear you saying, 'Unfair, you never told us anything about loss or profits on the sale of assets'? You're quite right, of course. There may be many happenings in accounts that are never quite explained. How do accountants know how to handle them? For one thing, they spend five years qualifying so they have a little more time then you to read up about such things. For another, they read the copious SSAPs – statement of standard accounting practice. But most of all, they get into the logic of where these items must appear and I am hoping that you, too, are now getting just that sort of logic from the accounts.)

Interest paid on the loan is 12 per cent of £90,000 = £10,800.

On the cash account the company has money – £139,200 – in the bank earning interest at 8 per cent, so interest received is £11,800 and the net interest is £300 received.

You will have realized that, if there are no penalties for repaying the loan early, and if Nephew Ltd has no other use of the cash, it is to the company's benefit to repay the loan from the surplus cash it will have by the end of the year. The company will then save the 4 per cent it is paying the bank for the privilege of borrowing its 'own money' (12 per cent paid on loan less the 8 per cent received on deposits).

Taxation is calculated at 42 per cent of the pre-tax profits. In the UK, the tax system does not allow depreciation to be used and adjusts the profit by adding back any depreciation that has been charged. This adjusted profit is then subjected to capital allowances that are allowable against the purchase of plant and equipment, buildings and vehicles, etc. (The capital allowances are defined by the Finance Act laid down by Parliament each year.) After all these calculations, we arrive at a taxable profit that the Inland Revenue is happy with and on which the company will be assessed. Many other countries handle things differently, so beware!

Dividends are now calculated on the issued capital of 100,000 ordinary shares.

Balance sheet

The land and buildings lease has been amortized for one more year, hence £20,000 was charged in the profit and loss account and the asset is reduced in value on the balance sheet to £100,000.

The plant and equipment has been sold.

The company bought another £15,000 worth of vehicles and then depreciated them at £4,000 over the year = a book value of £11,000. The original vehicles, which also cost £15,000, have now been depreciated over two years at £4,000 p. a. and thus have a book value of £7,000. (£11,000 + £7,000 = £18,000 as shown on the balance sheet.)

The interim dividend is usually declared halfway through the year and paid in the latter half of the year. It is therefore only the final dividend that remains outstanding at the year-end. A check on the cash account will reveal that cash of £16,000 was paid out on dividends, being the final dividend of last year (£8,000) and the interim dividend of this year (£8,000).

£10,000 was repaid on the loan.

An additional 20,000 ordinary shares were issued at the start of the year, so the ordinary share capital has gone up by 20,000 at the nominal (par) value of £1 = £20,000.

The company received £50,000 for the 20,000 £1 shares it issued, so it received a share premium of £30,000. It actually received cash, which it has spent or used by the end of the year. Hence reserves do not contain anything (Chapter 2). They merely show where the money came from that the company has now spent.

Cash flow statement

The adjustment for non-cash items includes:

- Amortization of the lease: £20,000.
- Depreciation of vehicles old and new: £8,000.
- Loss on sale of asset: £15,000.

The adjustments were necessary because, though the items were included on the profit and loss account and thus reduced profits, none of the above represents any cash leaving the company in 20X1.

The land and buildings were paid for at the start of 20XX and the lease is now being amortized via a book entry, ie no one is paying anyone another £20,000 cash each year for a lease for which you paid front-end cash of £140,000 (see Chapter 7).

A similar thing goes for £8,000 depreciation and for the loss on sale of assets, which did not involve anyone getting rid of £10,000 in cash.

Fixed assets decreased by the sale of the plant and equipment for £30,000, but increased at the purchase of more vehicles for £15,000 (making a net flow of cash into the company of £15,000).

Total debtors at the end of 20XX were £243,000 (trade debtors £240,000 plus non-trade debtors of £3,000) and are scheduled to be £242,700 (£236,700 + £6,000) at the end of 20X1, a decrease of £300.

Total creditors have moved from £61,000 (trade creditors £60,000 plus non-trade creditors £1,000) to £169,700 (£167,700 + £2,000 – twice the activity should attract twice the VAT), an increase of £108,700.

Stock has remained the same at £40,000.

Other items in 20XX had included the new loan of £100,000 less the loan repayment on the last day of the year of £(10,000). On the last day of 20X1 there was another loan repayment of £(10,000) leaving a balance of £80,000 shown on the balance sheet.

Budgets

A budget is very similar to a forecast. An organization looks at a period ahead and attempts to forecast its performance over that period of time. Huge problems can occur as companies get bigger and departmental responsibilities begin to take the place of the corporate strategy. I am still amazed by the number of companies that produce their budget or forecast on an uncoordinated departmental basis. In these companies, the following situation inevitably arises:

The sales department decide what they are going to be selling over the next twelve months and start producing forecasts of anticipated sales income based on the mix of products they anticipate selling.

The production department has to produce the goods so they have a shrewd idea of what the sales people are planning but temper it to their capacity restraints and their experience.

The delivery department learns of the total volume throughput and cost out their transport costs on the grounds of past history, upgraded for known changes.

The administration department produces its forecasts largely ignoring the other departments.

The accountants' department has enough to do with the impending year-end results and in collecting the budget figures and rattling them around in their computers without ensuring that all the bits are coordinated.

The end result is that sales succeed in selling products that go out of stock due to a differing production plan, or they sell a different mix that causes problems of delivery, or, the most frustrating scene of all, they will suddenly major on a product that was never planned without ensuring that everyone else updates their plans and budgets to accommodate the different sales schedule.

Production is therefore still producing according to its 'interpretation' of the original plan, and transport is still delivering according to its own interpretation. The administrators are still supporting a system that existed in previous years but is not fully relevant to the present day. The accountants, meanwhile, chase all the bits of paper and try to get them in the computer in time to produce a 30-page document alive and crawling with figures for all key managers to take home in their briefcases at night and bring back each day.

All departments can now firefight like mad through every day and try to 'make budget'. All departments can now work all the hours available to get the sales/production/deliveries/ paper/figures out on time; their marriages can collapse around them and they may never see their children grow up but, by Jove! they *will* get the task done. They will get as close to success as it is possible to be, and they will lose themselves in the process, feeling that they are doing a great job. Somehow they will try to make the budgeted 'bottom line' and when they do they will all sink back exhausted but triumphant. Then they can start all over again on the following year's budget and go through all this exciting anguish all over again.

If this sounds a harsh judgement then you would be mortified if I were to tell you that it is the normal situation in most companies, big and small, including multi million-dollar international trading corporations. The larger the company, the more departmentalized it becomes, the more tribal become its workers, staff and management and the more the solving of the departments' day-to-day problems becomes the sole reason for working.

It is little wonder that the good outside consultant can have such a beneficial effect when managements get so locked into their day-to-day problems that they fail to take the time to step back and really look at what they are doing each day and how the quality of the whole company's work might be improved. The solution, as always, is to keep it simple and return to basics.

A budget is an accurate forecast of a period ahead, usually twelve months. If performance is to be maximized then the 'restrictive factor' needs to be identified, ie what is the factor that stops the company producing the maximum return to its shareholders.

It might be the lack of a market for its products; the inability of the company to penetrate the available market; the lack of a product to match the market requirements; or the lack of production capacity to fulfil the market; or the lack of production quality to satisfy the market; or the lack of skilled staff to produce or design the product – or one of many other restrictive factors.

Once identified, the restrictive factor will control an element of forecasting. For instance, if nothing is done to improve a production restriction then sales must curb their activities on the products that use that facility in order to match the production capacity. They might be able to sell twice as many as can be produced and, in uncoordinated budgets, that is precisely what can occur, so all that sales effort is wasted. Customers are frustrated by late or even non-deliveries and everyone works all the hours that are available to satisfy a demand that could have been diverted to a product that production has the capacity to produce.

This is so even in market-led companies. It is no use selling a product you cannot produce or buy-in at a profit. In market-led companies it is often necessary to have a much more flexible type of production capacity but there are some production methods where the machinery in use makes it impossible to change in the short term.

The matching of sales to production capacity, or the matching of production to sales capacity, is the key to successfully putting together a cohesive plan for the twelve months ahead. As well as identifying the restrictive factors the company needs to identify the steps necessary to overcome those restrictions and, if necessary, build them into the plan. All of this can only be done by close cooperation between departments but, as stated above, the departmentalized company becomes very tribal in its outlook and there will be an awful lot of tribal skirmishes that will possibly cost someone their head before an amicable settlement comes about.

Once agreed by the board of directors, the twelve-month forecast becomes the budget or plan from which we measure progress over the period ahead.

The budget should not be used as a licence to spend whatever has been budgeted as expenditure for your department; rather it should be used as a 'measuring stick' of performance.

We know what the profit will be and what the company's cash requirements are if the budget is achieved, so by measuring deviations in actual results verses budget we can get an early warning of good or bad trends that are developing. Good management can then either correct the bad trends, build on the good or update their budgeted forecast for the trends that are being revealed. Really good management can achieve all three of those goals and move the company ever closer to maximum performance.

9

Measuring performance

In the earlier chapters we defined the major accounting documents and looked at how they are compiled and used. We also analysed them in some detail. In Chapter 7 we compiled the accounting reports for a business and in Chapter 8 we built a forecast for the year ahead using a cash account, a profit and loss account, a balance sheet and a cash flow statement. We then got that forecast approved by the board of directors and used it as a budget from which we could measure performance over the year ahead.

We have also considered the way these reports are used, within the accounting conventions, and by the occasional company that wishes to 'adjust' its figures to produce the required profits.

In this chapter we are going to look at the tools of the accountants' trade that allow us to measure performance of even the most complex business. Performance ratios, if understood correctly, can become the greatest aid to mastering finance that you will ever encounter. They are also the instrument panel to sound business management.

What are performance ratios? You have already been using some of them to measure performance in the earlier chapters. For example:

- return on capital employed;
- debtor days;
- creditor days;
- stock days;
- earnings per share;
- p/e.

The time has come to gather them together and make sure that we understand the significance of each, and then to apply them to a set of accounts and see what they reveal. We are going to separate the ratios into five groups:

- cash management;
- profit management;
- personnel;
- shareholders' interests;
- other.

The list cannot be exhaustive because of the changing nature of any dynamic business and the factors that affect it internally and externally. We are, however, going to look at a list of ratios that will prove of great help in any business.

Ratios on their own can tell us a great deal about a business, but their use is greatly enhanced by their regular production and analysis, either within the management accounts or annually in the case of published accounts. It is the analysis of the trends that are revealed that is all-important, along with the management quest to regularly improve each and every ratio.

If you can achieve that improvement, then your task of managing the business will meet with financial success, yours personally and the company's.

Ratios used intelligently, on a regular basis within a set of management reports, not only measure performance, but they can also be the keys to success. We will start with cash management:

Trade Debtor Days (Customers' credit days)	=	Trade debtors / Sales for the year	× 365
Trade Creditor Days (Suppliers' credit days)	=	Trade creditors / Purchases (or cost of goods sold)	× 365
Stock Days (Inventory days)	=	Stocks / Cost of goods sold	× 365
non-Working capital (Current ratio)	=	Current assets / Current liabilities	
Acid test ratio (Liquidity)	=	Current assets less stock / Current liabilities	

Debt/equity	=	Net borrowings
(Gearing)		Shareholders' funds
Interest cover	=	Operating (trading) profit
		Interest

Cash management ratios

Trade debtor days

| Trade debtor days | = | Trade debtors | × | 365 |
| (Customers' credit days) | | Sales for the year | | |

We have looked at debtor days in some detail in the earlier chapters. The above formula is an easier formula but more difficult to explain than the method used to calculate debtor days in the earlier chapters. Both give identical results.

Seasonal sales fluctuations can distort the above figure and a more accurate picture is given by the formula:

| Trade debtor days | = | Trade debtors | × | 90 |
| (Customers' credit days) | | Sales for the last 3 months | | |

This should be used on management accounts where the monthly figures are usually available. When looking at published accounts, however, only the 12-month results are available, hence the original formula is used.

Before we can judge what is a good or poor figure for debtor days we need to know the terms of trade of the particular company. If the company sells on 30-day terms then clearly the debtor days should be very close to 30 days. If the company sells on 60-day terms then the debtor days should be very close to 60 and so on. If the company has a variety of days included in its terms of trade then a little more investigation is necessary to come up with a weighted average against which the debtor days can be measured.

Debtor days probably represent the most appalling standard of mismanagement that occurs in business. Many organizations use enormous resources in the effort to sell their wares and then, once delivery is made, they walk away from any responsibility for collecting the payment from the customer.

Many company representatives haggle over every detail of price or quality, and the 'virtues' of their product or company, and then seal the deal with terms of trade at, say, 30 days. (It is common for them not to even mention the date that they would like to receive the cash from the sale.) When it comes to the company actually getting paid by those same customers, the general feeling is that it is always 'someone else's responsibility'.

Most companies pay commission and bonuses to their executives, staff and workers based upon orders taken or profits made, rather than cash received, a system that encourages poor cash management.

Commissions and bonuses should be paid on the contribution of each sale (sales price minus the variable elements of cost of sales) as opposed to being paid on the sales value, and then only on the invoices where the full payment has been received. This would dramatically improve the profitability and cash management. (If a further 2 per cent per month interest charge for late payment were to be deducted from the bonus or commission of the sales staff then debtor days would fall dramatically.)

In the UK, the payment cycle is often more than 78 days. The average terms of trade states less than 30 days, so the average customer is getting a month and a half (48 days) free credit. That is the average customer – goodness knows what the poor payer was enjoying.

Credit is costing the supplier up to 1.5 per cent per month and profit margins can be very tight indeed (far too tight to allow the average customer an extra 2.5 per cent on all the products).

If you are going to allow your customers to pay at 60 days or more then change your terms of trade to 60 days and allow the product costing to include a margin to cover the free credit you are allowing your customers. If your terms of trade are 30 days then collect the money at 30 days. It really isn't so difficult.

Our experience in this area reveals that once you let your customers go past 30 days it is difficult to rein them back. The longer the period of payment is past the terms of trade, the less inclined they are to pay.

If your terms are 30 days then it is essential that you vigorously chase them on day 30, 31, 32, etc, until payment is received or, better still, contract with them in such a way that they have no alternative but to pay on the due date. There are a lot of legitimate financial controls that can ensure payment on the due day in a way that is painless for all concerned.

If the company as a whole applies its mind to it, including altering the terms of trade and/or the required methods of payment where necessary, then it is possible to reduce the required customer payment period dramatically and achieve average debtor days within five days of the company's terms of trade.

Debtor days are a vital key management control and the current figure for his own business should be on the tip of the tongue of every manager. If you do not know what it is in your company then you are not managing cash!

And so to our management of our suppliers.

Trade creditor days

Trade creditor days = Trade creditors × 365
(Suppliers' credit days)   Purchases (or cost of goods sold)

Again, seasonal sales fluctuations can distort the above figure and a more accurate picture is given by the formula:

Trade creditor days = Trade creditors × 90
(Suppliers' credit days)   Purchases for last 3 months

This should be used on management accounts where the monthly figures are usually available. When looking at published accounts, however, only the 12-month results are available, hence the original formula is used.

The reason that cost of goods sold is shown as an alternative is that many sets of published accounts include the purchases made by the company as part of cost of goods sold, in which case the cost of goods sold is used. Occasionally that is not shown either and then sales must be used. If you are forced to use sales then you get a 'false result' – creditors are our suppliers and they relate to the cost price of our purchases, not the sell price of our goods (which is calculated after they have been marked up to cover the cost of labour, overheads and profit margins).

If you are looking at trends then the inaccuracy of the figure you take (cost of goods sold, or sales, instead of purchases) has less significance as long as you consistently use the same one. It is the movement in the ratio that is important.

If you are forced to use the sales figure instead of purchases and can find out, or estimate, the gross profit percentage of the particular company or industry then you will get a more accurate ratio. If you can establish the approximate level of purchases that are included in the company's cost of sales then the accuracy of the figure is enhanced.

What is a good or bad figure for creditor days? There is no one answer. For a start, we would need to know the terms of trade of the company's suppliers, but unless there were some exceptional circumstances then you would not expect creditor days to be less than the number of debtor days. Indeed, a golden rule for cash management is: *Never pay out until you have collected the money in.* Thus, as a general rule, creditor days should always be more than debtor days.

As with all ratios, it is not so much the figure itself that is important but it is the continual improvement of the ratio that should be the focus of management's attention and actions.

Stock days

Stock days (Inventory days)	=	$\dfrac{\text{Stocks}}{\text{Cost of goods sold}}$	x	365

Once again, in management accounts, it is possible to take out seasonal fluctuations in production levels with the formula:

Stock days   = Stocks   x 90
(Inventory days)   Last 3 months Cost of goods sold

Not so long ago, certainly within the time I have been involved in management, the object of a production unit was to produce as many items as possible within the resources available. Thus, downtime caused by machine breakdown, or lack of labour, had to be avoided at all costs and batch sizes were as large as possible because of these mysterious 'economies of scale' that the economic theorists told us about so often (but that are seldom found in practice). It was to gain economies of scale that the production units became ever larger and dominated landscapes and environments. Even governments fell for this theory and, since the 1960s, encouraged British businesses to merge and grow larger to 'become more competitive'.

The economies of scale that I learnt about as part of my accounting training are to me about as factual as the yeti or the Loch Ness monster, or even the beautiful mermaid from the frozen north. I've heard all about them, even sung about them in the bar of the rugby or cricket club, but never experienced the joy of witnessing one in real life.

The theory of maximum production was undoubtedly correct in the days of the mills of the 1800s, when we had unlimited cheap labour working all hours and a market that could absorb all we produced. Indeed, we paid people for what they produced on a system that became the 'piece-work' method of payment, which is still used in some places today. It was a very effective system and worked well when the workers knew that if they failed to produce to the required quality then they lost their job and starved. There was no welfare or alternative work; if they got thrown out of work they stole or they starved. Under such conditions the quality of their work was assured. You could put thousands of people in a factory and they would produce the level and quality of work you wanted.

Today, life is different. There is an educated work-force, mobility of labour and a global market, bringing with it global competition. The market for our products is no longer assured and the manufacturing base from which Great Britain dominated much of world trade for a hundred years or more has been eroded in all the traditional businesses.

The companies that have resulted from most of the mergers of the last 50 years, which were going to give us all these economies of scale, are now often uncompetitive because of low productivity. All kinds of reasons are given for the failure of the British manufacturing industry except the one that might be the most critical – the thinking that we could manage huge businesses in the late twentieth and early twenty-first centuries with a style of production and management that dates from the 1890s and the failure to change the production methods to meet the challenge of the 2000s and beyond.

What can be done? At the very least, change the whole basis of production.

In the old days (read 'in the present' for many companies) we used to maximize production, with little or no idle time, and then try to sell all we produced. If we had no rivals and an unlimited market then that would still be a great way of working. Unfortunately that situation hardly ever exists in today's global economy.

We can no longer enjoy the luxury of producing and then selling all that we produce. Today, we must sell and produce to order. We must become genuinely customer-responsive and 'market-led', which implies an ability to respond to both the market and the customer. This is fine if you can achieve it, but if many companies only took the trouble to listen and respond to their customers needs they would improve both their performance and their market impact dramatically.

Some companies claim to be 'market-led' and have nice mission statements and strategy documents defining themselves as such yet, upon investigation, you find that they are still production dominated and are using the management techniques of a century ago imposed on equipment of today. The equipment has been updated and would respond to different management techniques dictated by the market; the management thinking has not been updated and is often still in the dark ages.

There are two solutions to this dilemma:

One, get as close to the customer as possible to be able accurately to anticipate their orders and the date the orders will be required for delivery.

Two, shorten your production time.

Both these methods work extremely well but are perhaps beyond the scope of the contents of this book. It should, however, be an area of growing interest to managers in the twenty-first century as more and more companies realize the impact such methods can have on profitability and cash.

Most managers, when first confronted with the challenge of halving production times, throw their hands up in horror and advise (in words the author cannot always find in the dictionary) that it cannot be done and still make the same profits.

When asked what the average 'throughput' time is (ie the time it takes materials or products to go through the company from the moment of receipt to the moment they are delivered to the customer), most production managers can readily answer. The interesting question then to ask is whether they ever have a 'rush job', or an 'emergency job' to do. Most do from time to time, and most can get the 'rush job' through the factory in about a third of the time of their regular production (sometimes a lot less).

In such situations there is clearly scope for considerable reduction of stock inventories that normally consist of work-in-progress and finished goods (if you can produce in a third of the time then you only need about a third of the work-in-progress and the finished stock). In addition, the global economy we are now in allows most goods to be delivered within about 24 hours anywhere in the world. This has a two-fold effect, a reduction of your finished goods requirements and a reduction in your raw materials requirements (as replacement stock can be purchased on short delivery times).

Many companies are claiming to be 'market-led' but their production methods have not changed from those that owe their success to the days of the 'production-led'. A close look at many 'market-led' companies reveals that they are still as 'production-led' as ever they were.

Some of the leading indicators of the effectiveness of all the above are throughput times, delivery times, delays and, of course, the stock days ratio.

The target for stock days should be no longer than the 'rush-job' throughput time, plus the time it takes to get delivery of replacement raw materials.

Working capital

```
non-Working capital  =      Current assets
(Current ratio)             Current liabilities
```

Debtor days, creditor days and stock days are performance measures of different parts of the organization but all in turn contribute to the working capital ratio. The working capital is in the hands of the managers of the business and is thus an excellent guide to the day-to-day cash management performance.

A few years ago this ratio was often known as the 2~:~1 ratio. The realization that working capital ties up cash on which the company makes no profit whatsoever (the company only makes money when goods have been turned into sales and the money has actually been received from the customer) has led to the appreciation that the working capital ratio should be as low as possible commensurate with risk. What that is depends on the particular company and their suppliers' and financiers' assessment of risk.

The average figure throughout the UK for the working capital ratio was 1.6~:~1 (ie current assets are 1.6 times current liabilities) but, needless to say, if the company were managing cash successfully it should be a lot lower than the average.

Acid test ratio

```
Acid test ratio      =      Current assets less stock
(Liquidity)                 Current liabilities
```

The acid test ratio was considered alongside the working capital ratio as a 'test of liquidity' (the company's ability to pay its immediate bills). Many years ago this was known as the 1~:~1 ratio but, again, times have changed and the average has moved to 0.8~:~1.

What does this mean? We can illustrate the significance of all the ratios we've covered to date by looking at the type of ratios a leading food multistore would produce.

Cast your mind back to the last time you visited a food supermarket or multistore. How many days' stock (inventory) do you think was on the shelves and held in the stockroom at each location? Twenty years ago, a guess of about 21 days would have been fairly accurate because the stock includes cans of produce, bottles of beer and spirits, washing-up liquids, paper goods, hardware, clothing and household goods, etc, as well as the perishables that need replacing every day or so. Today, it is vastly different as such stores try to get their inventory down to less than one day, and many succeed.

Before the advent of computerized checkouts it was practically impossible, but now that the checkout can be linked directly to a central warehouse it is possible to start loading the replacement stock the very moment an item is being sold. Indeed, you can go one stage further. If you have a regular supplier for a particular type of product then you can let (or make) your supplier have a direct link into your central warehouse system and provide it with information on its products only. As the store sells its product then the central warehouse can be bypassed completely and the supplier can give a next-day delivery directly to the store.

More than one of my clients has made the necessary investment in such a computer linkage and, indeed, one such company has a direct satellite link with its customer's system that records every sale in stores throughout the USA. As a product is sold it is recorded on the central warehouse system and instantly on the supplier's computer link. The very same size, colour and pattern is sent on guaranteed next-day delivery by the supplier to a location anywhere throughout the USA and the store needs to keep only one day's stock, with no need of central support.

For the supplier to make money under such a system it must be able to support the operation and not just turn itself into the customer's inventory warehouse. Rather than hold the customer's stock for them it must halve, and then halve again, and keep on halving its own production batch sizes until the production response time equates as nearly as possible to the 'next-day delivery' required by their customer.

Is it worth all the hassle? Well, this customer is one of the largest store chains in the USA and, incredible as it seems, if you clear the multitude of work-in-progress out of the way and stop it interfering with the production that someone is willing to pay for, the cost of production under such a system actually falls.

If in doing so you also save the cost of your stores, storemen, security and warehousing, as well as the cost of all these items that are lying around waiting to be sold, then you get remarkable savings in cash, as well as the improvement in profitability.

Let us continue with the ratios of the efficient modern store.

What of debtor days? A lot of food stores will only take cash at the checkout tills or the 'Switch' debit cards that transfer the customer's cash directly into the store's bank account. Most try not to have 'account customers' but do accept cheques. The result is: debtors days = one day or less.

Creditor days are in the hands of the company's accountants and most have learnt from the stores that earlier took full advantage of this source of interest-free credit until they pushed their suppliers just too far. The store has to concede something for next-day delivery so it is usual to pay promptly for the privilege if the supplier asks them.

The fact that leaves me most incredulous from the many companies I have worked with is how few actually ask for the money, or for prompt payment, at the time they are making the contract with the customer.

There are also still a number of suppliers who fail to effectively chase for payment (as discussed above when describing debtor days) and you will find that the efficient store averages somewhere in the region of 50 to 60 creditor days without even trying to deliberately delay payment.

If we assume an average of 55 days for a food store, this is still a lot lower than the British average for all industries and many suppliers will think of 55 days as prompt payment (which really is a sign of how woefully weak their own cash management is).

Given the above then the efficient working capital begins to look like this:

CURRENT ASSETS	
STOCK	1 day
DEBTORS	1 day
CASH	?
CURRENT LIABILITIES	
CREDITORS	55 days
BANK OVERDRAFT	?
etc	

If we just think about the significance of the above, it means that items for sale arrive in the store today, are sold before the end of the day and the store owner has got the money in the bank by tomorrow.

Here comes the nice part: the store owner doesn't have to pay its suppliers for another 53 days (55 less the two just described) and some suppliers are going to think of it as a very good payer at that.

We can convert that into cash if we know the sales turnover of the type of company we are looking at and the gross margin that they would obtain. This type of company is turning over (sales) about £5 billion per annum, with a gross profit of about 10 per cent.

Given that knowledge we can convert the above into cash:

- One day's debtors = £5 billion, divided by 365 = £13.7 million.
- One day's stock would be the cost price of sales (90 per cent of one day's sales) = £12.3 million.
- Fifty-five days of creditors = 55 times one days' purchases (90 per cent of the sales) = £678.1 million.

Their working capital looks a little like the following:

CURRENT ASSETS	
STOCK	£12.3 million
DEBTORS	£13.7 million
CASH	?
CURRENT LIABILITIES	
CREDITORS	£678.2 million
BANK OVERDRAFT	?
etc.	

Now we can calculate how much of our suppliers' money resides in our bank account. As the sales cycle keeps going around (ie on day 55 we have another day's sales in our tills and ready for banking, from which we can pay our suppliers) we always have 53 days of suppliers' money lying idle in our bank account (if that is where you choose to leave it).

Fifty-three days at the cost of sales on a £5 billion turnover is £653,424,650, sitting in our bank account courtesy of our shrewd cash management. Not bad work if you can get it! We have actually banked the money the debtors have paid us thus allowing us the gross profit margin (our retail mark-up) of 10 per cent to spend in the meantime.

So, if we use the traditional accounting measures that are still being taught on many academic courses then we now have £653 million permanently residing in our bank account in order to have our acid test ratio at 1~:~1, ie current assets now equals current liabilities. (Stock at £12.3 million, debtors at £13.7 million, and cash at bank at £653 million = £679 million to cover the creditors of £678.2 million.)

The traditional accountants are happy because our acid test ratio is 1~:~1. The bank manager is happy because he or she can pay us 3 per cent on our deposit while charging someone else 12 per cent (18 per cent or more if on credit card) for borrowing our money. The academics are happy as they have been teaching the 1~:~1 and 2~:~1 ratios for years. Everyone's happy – or are they? The shareholders shouldn't be. That money should be earning more than 3 per cent by being invested in the business.

Accounting theory is all very well but if you were the owner of a foodstore with £653 million idly twiddling its thumbs in your bank account earning 3 per cent when you knew that if you used it to build another superstore somewhere, which would mean even more turnover (a store that costs £10 million to build turns over considerably more than £10 million per annum) at a gross margin of 10 per cent, and even more cash coming back into your own bank account, then it wouldn't take you long to use the new surplus to build some more glorious superstores. Thus you make even more profits and generate even more cash to build even more superstores. What a wonderful life, if only you can get your cash management correct!

Why don't we run every company this way? As long as gross profit, margins and overheads are well monitored and kept under control, the end-result of this cycle is a highly profitable company that is rapidly growing but with an appalling acid test ratio. (All the money that was in the bank account has now been spent on new stores so it is now in fixed assets.)

The acid test ratio will be less than 0.1~:~1 and not the 1~:~1 preferred by accounting theory. The new measurement of the acid test ratio and the working capital ratio is that they should be as low as possible commensurate with risk.

A lot of managers at this point in my lectures look at me with pity in their eyes at my simplicity and explain that it's all much more complicated than that. They tell me that suppliers are all aware of this use of their money and the prices charged to the foodstores include a margin to cover the delay in getting paid. This is all very laudable, but the problem is that I have yet to find the supplier who is able to add any margin whatsoever to a contract with a £5 billion foodstore company. The reverse is usually true.

The foodstore knows its buying power and squeezes every last bit of margin it can out of its suppliers. What's more, the suppliers can get paid at 55 days instead of the 78 days or more that other customers are taking, so they seldom complain, so that's another economic theory that doesn't work in practice.

In my experience this whole area of working capital control is much neglected in most companies and one in which there is constant demand for consultancy services.

If you look at the debtor list of your own company and consider how much cash can be generated by just reducing it to within five days of your terms of trade, you can see why this is. If you add the prospect of increasing the efficiency of the cash management throughout the organization and the additional cash that can be generated (at least five days off stocks and maybe even halving them, an additional five days on creditors, an increase in asset utilization by 5 per cent, etc) then it is little wonder that my work in line management and consultancy lays great emphasis on the management of cash and assets as well as profits.

Gearing

Debt/equity (Gearing)	=	Net borrowings / Shareholders' funds

There is more than one way of measuring the 'gearing' of a company, but the debt/equity is now about the most popular and the simplest. It is a measure of the proportion of borrowed capital to shareholders' capital.

The most commonly used alternative is a measure of net borrowings as a proportion of total funding:

> | Gearing | = | Net borrowings |
> |---|---|---|
> | | | Total borrowings + shareholders' funds |

Net borrowings indicate that any cash holdings or deposits the company has, along with any short-term deposits, are 'netted off' against the total borrowings (including overdrafts and other short-term borrowings as well as medium and long-term loans etc). The resultant figure is measured against the total shareholders' funds (share capital plus capital reserves and retained profits).

As a general rule, the suppliers of finance such as the banks begin to sleep uneasily when net borrowings exceed 60 per cent of the shareholders' capital for any prolonged period of time.

In good times with a buoyant economy, however, many banks fall over themselves to lend the big companies, conglomerates (companies who own a number of subsidiary companies or departments usually operating in diverse industries) and holding companies (companies that own the majority of shares in, or control of a number of subsidiary companies) all the cash they can for almost any acquisition they dreamed of. The result is the inevitable crash of many of these same organizations as soon as the economy gets tough.

Who's to blame, the banks who loaned out their money so carelessly, or the managers of the conglomerates and holding companies who used the loans so imprudently? You must decide, but in every case the signals are always given by the debt/equity ratio, the interest cover and the return on capital employed (although sometimes it is necessary to take a close look at some of the accountants' 'fair value' and 'goodwill' adjustments, as well as to take a hard look at their asset valuations).

You might ask why shareholders have auditors that often cost their company many millions each year, if the outsider has to look closely at these 'adjustments'. What is the auditor supposed to be doing? Most auditors try to cover their potential liability by asking all the right questions but, almost irrespective of the answers, still sign to say that the accounts give a 'true and fair view of the company' and then walk away with their fee. If that seems unjust then I'd be pleased to hear from the auditors how a certain media tycoon was able to 'adjust' his companies' figures over many years so efficiently that half his workers lost their pensions when he fell off his boat.

Interest cover

Interest cover	=	Operating (trading) profit
		Interest

Interest cover is another ratio that gives early warning of the company that is close to the slippery slope. The level of cover required depends on the type of industry and the economic situation.

A food shop, especially one with a reasonable share of the market, can be reasonably confident that it will continue to sell food in almost any economic situation as people must continue to eat, whereas a fashion outfitters might suffer in at least two ways. One, in that its products 'go out of fashion' and its sales drop away, and two, in times of economic hardship most people will make their fashion garment last just a little longer or put off buying a new one for some time.

The interest cover should therefore be far higher in the fashion trade than in the food store if risk is to be avoided. If your business is subject to cyclical fluctuations then you need a higher level of interest cover than the business that will always make approximately the same profit irrespective of all that happens around it.

Now we have looked at some of the measures of our performance as cash managers, I wonder how your company measures up. Remember the name of the game is continually to improve the ratios month in and month out. Have a look at your company's annual report and accounts and see if you can work out the cash management ratios. When you've done so, make a few criticisms of them: are they good, or bad? Could they be improved and, if so, how? And so on.

Profit management ratios

Return on capital employed % (ROCE)	=	$\dfrac{\text{Operating profit} \times 100}{\text{Capital employed}}$
Gross profit on sales % (Gross margin)	=	$\dfrac{\text{Gross profit} \times 100}{\text{Sales}}$
Operating margin (Return on sales – ROS)	=	$\dfrac{\text{Operating profit} \times 100}{\text{Sales}}$
Overheads %	=	$\dfrac{\text{Overheads} \times 100}{\text{Gross profit}}$
Stock turnover	=	$\dfrac{\text{Cost of goods sold}}{\text{Stocks}}$
Asset turnover	=	$\dfrac{\text{Sales}}{\text{Capital employed}}$
Revenue per unit	=	$\dfrac{\text{Sales}}{\text{Number of units}}$
Gross profit per unit	=	$\dfrac{\text{Gross profit}}{\text{Number of units}}$
Operating profit per unit	=	$\dfrac{\text{Operating profit}}{\text{Number of units}}$

Let us start with the ratio that you will often see described as the *primary ratio*.

Return on capital employed

ROCE	=	$\dfrac{\text{Operating profit} \times 100}{\text{Capital employed}}$

The capital employed (shareholders' funds plus long-term borrowings) is also often displayed under the heading of total assets less current liabilities. It is a measure of the amount of money, or value, the managers of the business have had under their control. Some of the money will have already been spent on long-term assets (fixed assets) and some on the provision of working capital (eg inventory and debtors) and some may be cash in the bank.

Whatever shape or form it is in, the capital employed is taken as the amount of value that the managers have (or have had) under their control.

The shareholders and the providers of loans need to see that the company makes sufficient return on the money employed in the business (the capital employed) to service those loans (be able to pay the interest and make the repayments on the loan when due) and still provide a profit.

What is a sufficient return? Certainly more than the shareholder can make from depositing those same funds elsewhere, such as a bank, building society or some other reasonably secure place.

If you put your money in a bank, you can get it back pretty much when you like and it will earn reasonable interest (16 per cent was achievable in the early 1990s). If you put your money into shares then you cannot be sure to get all your money back (shares go down as well as up and companies go broke) but you will probably receive a dividend and you will own a part of a company that might grow larger by successfully using all the retained profits.

There needs to be a measure that the shareholder or any other interested party can use to see what return the managers of a business are achieving for their shareholders. The most popular measure is the return on capital employed (ROCE) or, in the case of a company or division that is part of a larger group, return on investment (ROI), investment being the amount of value the group has tied up in that particular company or division.

ROCE (return on capital employed) is measured by taking the operating profit (which is the profit before interest and tax – PBIT) and expressing that as a percentage of the capital employed.

As the operating profit is the profit before interest and tax then the rate of return you are looking for under this ratio needs to be better than the rate of interest the company is paying, ie if you are borrowing money and it is invested in the business in fixed or working capital then the company must be making more on the use of that money than it is paying in interest. If you only make a ROCE of 10 per cent but are borrowing money at 15 per cent then you are paying the bank more in interest than you make on the money you borrowed. In such situations it is better not to have borrowed the money in the first place. (This is all so obvious, yet curiously it is overlooked by so many managers and their companies – and by their shareholders.)

To emphasize the point again, the return on capital employed needs to be higher than the highest cost of borrowings. If it isn't then don't borrow the money.

Unfortunately, when interest rates increase, the ROCE of many highly leveraged companies (companies with high borrowings) is often significantly below the cost of interest they are required to pay on their borrowed money.

Cash generation from within a company is a much neglected management skill, and in the last recession many of the highly leveraged companies simply did not generate sufficient cash to pay their interest. Of those that did, many had insufficient cash left to meet the repayments of the money they had borrowed at the due dates, hence the record number of liquidations throughout those years – a situation that will be repeated at the time of the next great recession.

Gross profit on sales

Gross profit on sales %   = $\dfrac{\text{Gross profit} \times 100}{\text{Sales}}$
(Gross margin)

Published accounts do not always give sufficient information to enable the reader to calculate the gross profit and so this ratio is not often included in reports and on databases. Gross profit on sales (gross profit percentage) can, however, be a vital management tool to concentrate attention on the areas of the business that need it.

When looking at trends, if the gross profit percentage falls, it indicates problems near the 'sharp end' of the business. Gross profit is calculated before all the overhead expenses, interest and tax, so those can be ignored when looking for reasons that lie behind any change in the gross profit percentage and concentration can be focused on the sales and direct costs.

If any of the direct costs (materials, direct labour or factory costs) have increased without sales prices increasing then it will adversely effect the gross profit percentage, and the movement in this ratio can be an early indicator to management of such increases.

If direct costs were steady then a movement in selling prices or discounts given to customers would also cause this ratio to change.

If the cause of change in the gross profit percentage proves to be none of the above then have a look at the sales mix.

Many companies persist in the outmoded method of paying sales commissions based on sales turnover, ie the total value of the sales instead of sales contribution, and this encourages the maximization of the sales revenue rather than the maximization of the profitable sales revenue. As a result, many companies have found to their cost that the sales revenue has stayed high but that profit has 'disappeared'. Upon investigation it often turns out that the disappearance has been caused by a move by their customers away from the company's more profitable products into the less profitable, or to higher discounts being given, with the result that the 'bottom line' shrank without anyone being aware of the reasons.

Operating margin

Operating margin (Return on sales – ROS)	=	$\dfrac{\text{Operating profit} \times 100}{\text{Sales}}$

The operating margin ratio is used by many companies as a panacea for all things and some very poor and quite incorrect management decisions are made in the name of ROS (operating margin).

This ratio is a useful indicator but only when used in conjunction with the others contained within this chapter. Get those correct and the operating margin will look after itself.

To use one ratio, as many managers do, to the exclusion of all others, is to mismanage. It's like a pilot trying to fly an aircraft by looking at only one instrument. (Never mind the fact that the fuel gauge shows empty, and the altimeter is dropping rapidly, look, we're going at 600 miles per hour, it's a triumph, we've never gone that fast before!) Yet many companies do just that. This type of management is a symptom of the approach that plagued much of British industry in the 1970s and 80s. ('Rather than take the time to master finance we'll just manage the bottom line.')

If the gross profit percentage slips then it is likely that the operating margin (ROS) will also slip as a smaller gross profit will result in a smaller operating profit unless drastic trimming takes place on the overheads. However, there are many occasions when the gross profit percentage stays firm but the ROS reduces, and this can be due to the volume of trade decreasing to a level that can no longer support the same overheads.

Overheads

$$\text{Overheads \%} = \frac{\text{Overheads} \times 100}{\text{Gross profit}}$$

Many companies prefer to measure overheads against sales, but my strong recommendation is to measure overheads against the gross profit. There are two reasons for this thinking.

Overheads are, by nature, costs that are affected by time, not by throughput. Salaries are paid on a weekly or monthly basis and once staff are recruited they are on the payroll almost irrespective of the level of sales the company makes. Premises costs are commitments for the period ahead (ie time not throughput). A similar argument can be made for all the costs that are listed as overheads (otherwise they might be considered as direct costs and listed as part of the cost of sales).

It is for all these reasons, and the argument presented in the earlier chapters that the only reason for incurring overheads is to enhance the gross profit, that the ratio should be measuring the overheads as a percentage of the gross profit.

Stock turnover

| Stock turnover | = | Cost of goods sold |
| | | Stocks |

This ratio is commonly used on databases but is far less significant to most non-financial managers than the stock days (explained above in cash management). Stock turnover is a less effective ratio than one that carefully monitors the number of days of stock the company has and calls for an explanation even if the increase is just one day.

Asset turnover

| Asset turnover | = | Sales |
| | | Capital employed |

Many companies in the 1980s 'bought' the improvements they showed in increasing the earnings per share through making acquisitions and then writing off the cost of goodwill by reducing their reserves. This unfortunate (though quite legal) manoeuvre distorted the performance of management and in some cases nearly bankrupted the company.

If 'goodwill' and 'fair-value' write-offs and adjustments are added back into the balance sheet then the asset turnover is a good indicator of sales growth in relation to the asset base. Has the company been able to improve the sales performance from existing assets or has it been forced to 'buy' the additional sales it is enjoying? In the same way, an indication is available to see whether the company has reduced the asset base in times of falling sales as no longer needed to support that level of activity.

Revenue per unit

| Revenue per unit | = | Sales |
| | | Number of units |

The unit used in this group of ratios should be one that is a critical measure of the company. In a manufacturing company it might be a unit of production. In a retail organization it could be a square foot of display space, or revenue per customer (or both). In a trucking company it could be revenue per truck, or revenue per truck/mile and so on.

The revenue per unit is less important than the gross profit per unit (contribution per unit is the most useful ratio of all the unit measures) but revenue per unit is usually the easiest to measure and, providing you keep the gross profit percentage and overhead percentage under control via the other ratios, then you can be reasonably certain that performance overall will be satisfactory and on target.

Gross profit per unit

Gross profit per unit	=	$\dfrac{\text{Gross profit}}{\text{Number of units}}$

Gross profit per unit (ie the gross profit we are making on each unit of production, square foot of display space, customer or truck, etc) is another ratio that, if on target, will help to ensure a successful financial result to the year's activities.

Operating profit per unit

Operating profit per unit	=	$\dfrac{\text{Operating profit}}{\text{Number of units}}$

Another 'bottom-line' figure, and my reservation on 'bottom-line' measures is by now duly recorded. Ultimately, it is the operating profit that is the key measure of management's abilities, but as a control ratio operating profit per unit is limited. Get the others right and this one will be satisfactory.

Personnel ratios

A large proportion of most companies' expenditure is spent on personnel, so the personnel ratios can be vital to ensuring the continuing well being of any organization.

The unfortunate fact about personnel management in practically any organization is that personnel are recruited to fill perceived vacancies rather than to make a profit.

At this point, I sense a swelling indignation from personnel managers the world over, but experience reveals that the question 'In which way will this person being recruited increase the operating profit, or the earnings per share of this company?' is hardly ever asked. Yet this is the sole reason for a profit-making company employing anyone.

We so often recruit because a job exists for which there is a vacancy, without asking whether that job really needs to be done. One frequently finds a task being undertaken, which is extremely important to the department that is undertaking it, that has no actual practical benefit to the profitability of the company whatsoever.

All of the per capita ratios are vital measures of the use of personnel and their productivity:

Sales per capita	= Sales / Number of (full-time) employees
Gross profit per capita	= Gross profit / Number of (full-time) employeees
Operating margin per capita	= Operating profit / Number of (full-time) employees
Employee costs per capita	= Total employee costs / Number of (full-time) employees
Overheads per capita	= Total overheads / Number of (full-time) employees

Units per capita	=	Number of units
		Number of (full-time) employees
Indirect ratio	=	Number of (full-time) direct employees
		Number of (full-time) indirect employees
Capital employed per capita	=	Capital employed
		Number of (full-time) employees

Sales

Sales per capita	=	Sales
		Number of (full-time) employees

The sales revenue per capita is less important than the gross profit per capita (contribution per capita is the most useful ratio of all the capita measures) but revenue per capita is usually the easiest to measure. Providing you keep the gross profit percentage and overhead percentage under control via the other ratios then you can be reasonably certain that you are achieving the required overall performance.

Gross profit

Gross profit per capita	=	Gross profit
		Number of (full-time) employees

Gross profit per capita is the key to the successful use of the company's personnel. It is another ratio that, if on target, will help to ensure a successful financial result to the year's activities. Each new person recruited must increase the gross profit by considerably more than the cost of the person. For the maximum utilization of employees, and as a means of continually focusing management on the reason for their role in the company or organization, this measure should be used every time a new recruit is suggested, particularly when the apparent vacancy is not a factory, sales or direct worker.

Operating margin

Operating margin per capita = $\dfrac{\text{Operating profit}}{\text{Number of (full-time) employees}}$

The history of the latter part of the twentieth century is one of declining direct costs as technology replaces the old labour-intensive production techniques, and of increasing overhead costs for reasons that are not apparent unless you apply some of Parkinson's well-known laws.

The only reason for employing anyone in a profit-making organization is to make more profit, and operating profit per capita is a measure to show that this proportion is not declining with each new recruitment.

Employee costs

Employee costs per capita = $\dfrac{\text{Total employee costs}}{\text{Number of (full-time) employees}}$

We constantly read in the newspapers the speeches of politicians and academics who apparently believe, and try to convince us, that the problem with Britain and other western countries is high wage costs and that it is essential that 'the workers' must restrain their pay increases to below inflation.

This concept, that the blame for most of the country's economic ills lies with the labour force rather than where it actually belongs (on mismanagement by those in charge of governing the country), is one that I challenge. I give much greater emphasis to the productivity and profitability that is generated by the labour force as a means of reward, rather than a percentage increase on last years income.

It is not how much you pay your workers that matters but how much they produce for you per £1 (euro, $1, etc) of labour cost, and that is as much dependent upon motivation and direction (ie the skills of the management) as it is upon the actual sum paid. Under any reward system, however, we need to measure the average employee costs per capita.

Employee costs would include salaries and wages, social services and welfare costs, plus any other benefits made by the company including pension provisions and so on.

Overheads

Overheads per capita	=	Total overheads
		Number of (full-time) employees

Overheads are the costs that seem to be most easy to incur in an organization and the most difficult to get rid of. They are often related to the perceived needs of staff and support operations and the measure of overheads per capita will monitor and help to keep these costs in focus. There is often a correlation between overheads and the number of people who are employed. An example is that space has to be found for the new employee, and a desk, and support operations might need to be extended until support staff are needed to support the non-direct employees and managers and a mini- or complete bureaucracy is established that adds not a penny to the profits of the business.

Units per capita

Units per capita	=	Number of units
		Number of (full-time) employees

If the company is in manufacturing then its prime purpose is to manufacture to its customers' orders and sell products at a profit. There should be some correlation between the number of people employed and the number of units produced. Similarly, one would expect a correlation between the number of people employed in a retail store and the number of customers serviced. This is another of the early warning ratios that indicate the relationship between employees and productivity is improving or deteriorating.

Indirect ratio

Indirect ratio	=	Number of (full-time) direct employees
		Number of (full-time) indirect employees

This is a classic ratio. It highlights the direction the company is taking. It also emphasizes the trend in established companies to lose sight of the reason for their existence.

In companies that have grown to a reasonable size, management often begins to recruit a plethora of secretaries, clerks, and non-productive professionals (usually a combination of accountants, solicitors and administrators, many of whom have to have their supporting secretaries, clerks, etc). When these people have been recruited they have to do something to justify their existence and high salaries, so they produce very important memos and attend meetings, most of which stop them and other people from working. The result is the modern plethora of more and more meetings, which would be unnecessary if the management really understood the technique of delegated authority, and less and less real work. More and more of the profits that rightly belong to the shareholders are going to support operations that often contribute little to the successful operation of the company (indeed sometimes get in the way of success).

One should be able to assume that a company's managers are employed to maximize profits and the return to shareholders and, if that is true, then the only reason for employing anyone is to increase that profit.

The indirect ratio can therefore be very revealing. A particular mill that was no longer profitable can illustrate its use. When I went along to help, the very first thing to hit me was that there were 60 people working on the knitting machines and 180 people supporting them in some capacity or other (only 10 of whom were in sales). It didn't take a genius to work out where all their profit was going.

Capital employed

Capital employed per capita =	Capital employed
	Number of (full-time)
	employees

Not a ratio to make management leap up and act as so many of the others should, but a useful indicator of the amount of investment made by the company in assets per person.

Other personnel ratios

There is a multitude of other ratios, all as important for measuring and improving performance as those above, but they tend to be trade-related rather than applied to all companies. For example:

- Sales per square foot – used where floor area is a significant factor as in retailing and showrooms, etc.
- Gross profit per square foot.
- Sales per salesperson.
- Production per worker.
- Gross profit per £ (euro, $, etc) of marketing cost.
- Gross profit/admin and support.
- Sales/machine hours.
- Gross profit per container.

There is no limit to these and you can no doubt think of many that might be effective in your own industry.

The secret of ratios is to find those that allow you to exercise control without having to do lots of complicated arithmetic or investigation.

Shareholders' interests

We have discussed some of these ratios in earlier chapters but it is worth restating them in this section. They are the most commonly used measures by which the shareholders determine if their investment is worthwhile and ultimately, therefore, whether the company is worth keeping going. Examples are:

Earnings per share	=	After-tax profit
		Number of ordinary shares issued
Price/earnings (p/e)	=	Market price per share
		Earnings per share
Dividend yield	=	Dividend per share
		Market price per share
Dividend cover	=	Earnings per share
		Dividend per share

Earnings per share

Earnings per share	=	After-tax profit
		Number of ordinary shares issued

This ratio is the one most often quoted and illustrated in the company's report and accounts. It is calculated simply by dividing the after-tax profit (sometimes called after-tax earnings) by the number of ordinary shares that have been issued. Traditionally, the after-tax earnings have been adjusted by the addition or subtraction of extraordinary items.

Extraordinary items are items of income or expenditure that are thought unlikely to re-occur and that are not incurred in the usual course of trading. The intention of having a heading for extraordinary items is that such costs could be shown on the profit and loss account without distorting the performance for the year as shown by the operating profit.

HOW TO MASTER FINANCE

Unfortunately, however, a number of companies describe costs that should be included in the normal items of the profit and loss account as extraordinary and then use the extraordinary items to disguise the true state of their performance. This allows them to report higher earnings per share by using the after-tax profits adjusted for extraordinary items.

Reorganization costs are used in a similar way. They may have a legitimate use in some cases, for instance following a takeover where reorganization may be beneficial to all. However, all too often they are used to disguise the results of poor management decisions in the past that have led to the write-off of considerable sums of money from the profit and loss account under this heading.

There are many moves afoot to have this practice changed and it will be interesting to hear all the arguments put forward for the retention of this quaint 'adjustment'.

Price/earnings

Price/earnings (p/e)	=	$\dfrac{\text{Market price per share}}{\text{Earnings per share}}$

The market price of a share depends on supply and demand (although both can be stimulated with the odd rumour or two). When you strip its mystique away, the stock exchange is similar to a great fruit market and stockbrokers are really the barrow boys of this world. In the same way as when apples are in great supply the price drops in order that the sellers can get rid of all their stock, so a share price falls if everyone starts to sell their shares. When there is a demand for apples that exceeds the supply the price goes up, and it is the same with shares.

The market price for shares fluctuates daily or, indeed, many times throughout each day as deals are made. The earnings per share is calculated on the last set of published accounts for a company. There is, therefore, a time lag between the two halves of this ratio.

People generally buy shares in the hope of earning money on them over the period ahead (either because the share price is going to increase and thus allow them to sell the shares again at a profit, or because they hope to enjoy good dividends in the future). The demand for a share is, therefore, based on the buyer's assessment of the future prospects for that company.

So, a high p/e ratio reflects the fact that the purchasers of the share are expecting the price to rise and/or expecting the company to produce better results in the future than it did last year (the year in which the earnings per share is calculated). A low p/e ratio indicates the reverse – that buyers are expecting a drop in share price in the future and/or a drop in earnings (after-tax profits) over future years.

The higher the p/e ratio the more expectation people have that the company will increase future profits, or that a predator will make a take-over bid for it thus pushing the future share price up above that at which it is presently trading.

Dividend yield

Dividend yield	=	Dividend per share
		Market price per share

The dividend is the amount of the earnings (after-tax profits) that is distributed (given as a dividend) to the shareholders and thus the amount of cash they actually receive in return for owning the shares of the company. It is usually paid twice a year. The interim dividend is 'declared' by the board of directors when the half-year financial results are known and is normally paid in the latter half of the financial year. The final dividend is 'proposed' by the directors and then 'approved' at the annual general meeting of the members (the shareholders).

The interim and final dividends are added together and the resultant total is divided by the market price per share to give dividend yield. If multiplied by 100, the dividend yield will then be expressed as a percentage return on your money and can be compared with the return you would get from the other places you could deposit your funds.

You must keep in mind, however, that the dividend per share is only a part of the earnings per share and thus the company is retaining some of your money (assuming you are the share-holder), presumably for future growth. The problem is that when the future arrives you may well find that the directors still feel the need to hold on to your money for future growth and, if they persuade enough shareholders to back their judgement, you might never enjoy the fruits of all the earnings they have retained. As the wise old man once said: 'Always beware the promise of jam tomorrow but costs today.'

Dividend cover

Dividend cover	=	Earnings per share
		Dividend per share

Dividend cover is based on the last set of accounts and reflects the amount of earnings that are given to the shareholder as a dividend (ie cash that they can spend).

The shareholders that have invested because of the need for additional income would probably be happiest with a company where most of the earnings are distributed as dividends. In a company with low-dividend cover (ie that distributes most of its earnings as dividend), if earnings fluctuate then the likelihood is that dividends will also fluctuate (although this can be alleviated by use of the revenue reserve shown in the balance sheet).

A company may distribute by way of a dividend the revenue reserve (ie the retained profits of that year or of preceding years). Thus it can declare a dividend and distribute it in years when it makes no profit, providing there are retained profits from previous years.

There are restrictions on the repayment of any capital reserve or share capital.

Other shareholders' ratios

There is a multitude of other shareholders' ratios and tools of the trade that would require a book of their own to describe. The few we have featured here are to be found in the City columns of most newspapers and are used by many shareholders along with: debt/equity (the comparison of the company's net borrowings with the amount of money invested in the company by the shareholders); interest cover (the number of times the interest payments are covered by the PBIT) and some of the others featured above. It would be nice to think that the shareholders are influenced by all the ratios shown above but, alas, many of them are neglected, often to the peril of shareholder, manager and employee alike.

Use of the ratios

We've discussed a number of key ratios – but how are they used? The accounts of any company may be analysed to reveal most of the ratios and there are many organizations that do precisely that for you. Some even publish books of inter-company comparisons showing the average ratios for each type of trade. Others have the accounts and ratios of thousands of companies available on computer disk or database and available (at a fee) for quick reference.

Ratios are the method used to get a feel for the performance of the management of different companies and different industries. They comprise a manager's toolbox that is full of vital tools. They are the flight deck instruments of the pilots of the company.

The best way to understand their use is to calculate them for yourself and see what they tell you. Let us go back to the accounts of Nephew Ltd that we produced in Chapter 8. If you really want a full understanding of ratios then it's time for you to work out all the above ratios for Nephew Ltd over the 20XX actual accounts and the 20X1 forecast.

Remember: you learn most by doing, so have a go for yourself first and then check your solution with that given overleaf.

Performance ratios for Nephew Ltd				
PERFORMANCE RATIOS		**20XX**		**20X1**
CASH MANAGEMENT				
DEBTOR DAYS	243.0 / 960.0	92 days	242.7 / 1920.0	46 days
CREDITOR DAYS	61.0 / 680.0	33 days	169.7 / 1360.0	46 days
STOCK DAYS	40.0 / 715.0	20 days	40.0 / 1446.0	10 days
non-**WORKING CAPITAL**	283.0 / 264.4	1.07	433.0 / 244.7	1.76
ACID TEST RATIO	243.0 / 264.4	0.92	393.0 / 244.7	1.61
DEBT/EQUITY	261.8 / 104.6	250.%	= / 226.7	–
INTEREST COVER	94.4 / 38.2	2.5	154.4 / 0.3	–
PROFIT MANAGEMENT				
RETURN ON CAPITAL EMPLOYED	94.4 / 194.6	48.5%	154.4 / 306.3	50.4%
GROSS PROFIT %	245.0 / 960.0	25.5%	474.0 / 1920.0	24.7%
OPERATING MARGIN	94.4 / 960.0	9.8%	154.4 / 1920.0	8.0%
OVERHEADS %	150.6 / 245.0	61.5%	319.6 / 474.0	67.4%
STOCK TURNOVER	715.0 / 40.0	17.9	1446.0 / 40.0	36.2
ASSET TURNOVER	960.0 / 459.0	2.1	1920.0 / 553.1	3.5
REVENUE PER UNIT	960.0 / 100.0	£9.60	1920.0 / 200.0	£9.60
GROSS PROFIT PER UNIT	245.0 / 100.0	£2.45	474.0 / 200.0	£2.37
OPERATING PROFIT PER UNIT	94.4 / 100.0	£0.94	154.4 / 200.0	£0.77

PERSONNEL RATIOS

£(000)s

SALES per Capita	$\frac{960.0}{6}$	£160.00	$\frac{1920.0}{11}$	£174.55
GROSS PROFIT per Capita	$\frac{245.0}{6}$	£40.80	$\frac{474.0}{11}$	£43.09
OPERATING PROFIT per Capita	$\frac{94.4}{6}$	£15.73	$\frac{154.4}{11}$	£14.04
EMPLOYEE COSTS per Capita	$\frac{57.0}{6}$	£9.50	$\frac{127.0}{11}$	£11.55
OVERHEADS per Capita	$\frac{150.6}{6}$	£25.10	$\frac{319.6}{11}$	£29.05
UNITS per Capita	$\frac{100}{6}$	16.66	$\frac{200}{11}$	18.18
INDIRECT Ratio	$\frac{4}{2}$	2.0	$\frac{8}{3}$	2.7
CAPITAL EMPLOYED per Capita	$\frac{194.60}{6}$	£32.43	$\frac{306.3}{11}$	£27.85

Other ratios

If we had more information about the trade carried on by Nephew Ltd, we would be able to evolve a number of critical ratios that would help enhance management's performance. Within the context of this exercise we must leave you to think through other ratios that would serve the purpose of enhancing performance and monitoring progress.

Shareholders' Ratios

Earnings per Share	$\dfrac{32.60}{80.0}$	41p	$\dfrac{89.70}{100.0}$	90p
Price/Earnings (p/e)	$\dfrac{2.50}{0.41}$	6.1	$\dfrac{7.80}{0.90}$	8.7
Dividend Yield %	$\dfrac{10}{2.50}$	4.0%	$\dfrac{18}{7.80}$	2.3%
Dividend Cover	$\dfrac{32.6}{8.0}$	4.1	$\dfrac{89.7}{18.0}$	5.0

Now we've calculated the ratios, what can they tell us? Remember that in the normal way of using them you would not have had the benefit of completing all the accounts as you did in Chapter 8 and so you would be using the ratios to give you a feel for the performance of the management of the company.

We would normally attempt to get the ratios for at least three years' results (and preferably five) before attempting to interpret trends, but to do so within the context of this book would be to snow you under with figures. Therefore, we are simply comparing the actual of 20XX with the forecast for 20X1 for Nephew Ltd. Our hope is that when you have finished this chapter you will get your own company's report and accounts for the last five years (or the accounts of any other company you are interested in) and produce as many of the ratios as you can – and then see if you can determine the trends they show.

Analysis of ratios for Nephew Ltd

Cash management

	20XX	20X1
Debtor Days	92 days	46 days

Clearly there has been success in getting the customers (debtors) to pay more quickly. The reduction in the time spent waiting for your money to arrive from your account customers has resulted in considerable cash benefits to the company.

Had this improvement not been made then the company would have been forced to provide cash to cover 92 days of debtors on the much higher sales revenues forecast for 20X1 (sales of £1,920,000 at 92 days = £483,945 of trade debtors, an increase of £240,945 over last year). This cash would have had to be found from somewhere at whatever overdraft rates are in existence.

Creditor Days	33 days	46 days

The extension of the time being taken to pay the suppliers (creditors) from a very prompt 33 days to 46 days (this would still be considered as a prompt payment by many organizations) enables the company to hold on to cash longer and thus help to reduce any reliance on bank borrowings etc.

The trade suppliers (creditors) have supplied an additional £108,700 of finance for next year.

Stock Days	20 days	10 days

The halving of stock days not only reduces the amount of cash that is 'uselessly' tied up in the working capital of the company but, if carried through into batch sizes and producing to orders rather than to stock, then it might also lead to more vigorous production controls and with it the ability to respond more readily to customers' needs.

If stock had stayed at 20 days then another £40,000 would have needed to be borrowed just to put the products on the shelf or in the warehouse.

non-Working Capital ratio	1.07	1.76

The efficient, modern company is trying to get this ratio negative, ie well below 1. The movement in debtor days, creditor days and stock days should have resulted in a lower working capital ratio, yet the ratio has increased from 1.08 to 1.76.

The reason is that the company is sitting on the cash that it has generated and has it in the bank earning interest at 8 per cent. While this might allow the directors (and the banks) to feel secure, if it isn't going to be used within the company then it is an indication of weak management. If you look at the return on capital employed you will see that if the money had been reinvested in the business at a similar rate of return then it would have earned 50.4 per cent in 20X1 instead of the 8 per cent it is getting in the bank.

If the company has no use for the money then it would be better to feed it back to the shareholders by way of dividends and let them use it on something that will earn them more than bank deposit rates if they so wish. (Care must be taken, however, over the current legislation and you must beware of legal restraints and taxation on dividends if this course of action appeals to you.)

The non-working capital ratio should be as low as possible, commensurate with risk. In the 1900s the traditional accountants and bankers would have considered a ratio of 1.07 or even 1.76 as far too low, particularly when the high borrowings of the company are taken into account (debt/equity of 250 per cent).

In 20X1, the entire overdraft has been repaid and if the terms of the long-term loan allowed early repayment then £80,000 of the cash could be used to repay that (saving the £10,800 in interest charges).

If it had been possible to distribute the rest of the cash as a dividend then the shareholders would have received another 70p a share in dividends. (Cash at the end of 20X1 equalled £150,300, of which we're suggesting that £80,000 could be repaid on the loan at the end of the year, leaving £70,000 to be distributed and £200 retained in the bank. £70,000 divided by the number of ordinary shares issued – 100,000 – equals 70p a share.)

If such a repayment of loan and distribution of surplus cash by way of a dividend had been implemented then the current assets would be reduced by the £159,000 we have just parted with and the non-working capital ratio would have been £282.9~:~£244.7, ie 1.16~:~1.

A 1.16, non-working capital ratio would be much closer to the heart of the company accountant who wants to see all assets (including cash) working for the shareholders, but would frighten many a manager and banker who likes the company to sit on cash in case they need it. If the company's strategy and planning is so vague that they have to tie up assets 'in case of need' then the managers should seriously think about whether they are actually managing the company or just sitting on resources.

Acid Test Ratio	0.92	1.61

This ratio is sometimes called the liquidity ratio and is usually measured alongside the non-working capital ratio. Most of the same remarks apply to both. Nephew Ltd is run with a relatively low stock requirement. In companies where the reverse is true then this is one of the ratios that indicates whether problems would be created in the company's ability to pay all its short-term bills if the short-term suppliers of cash or credit closed up on them.

It can be seen from the above that in 20XX the company was pretty well safe with nearly all its current liabilities covered by the liquid funds that are included in the acid test ratio. In 20X1 the large holdings of cash make it is super-safe, but read the remarks at the end of the non-working capital ratio.

A high acid test ratio again indicates cash tied up in the business and not working for the shareholders. If the loan repayment and dividend distribution suggested under the working capital ratio above were to be enacted then the acid test ratio would have been 0.99~:~1, still too high but an improvement on the 1.61 that will otherwise result from the company's plans for 20X1.

Debt/Equity	250.%	–

Lenders of money to a company would normally wish the shareholders to be at greater risk than the lenders themselves. The doctrine of limited liability (ie when Ltd or plc appears after the company's name) means that the liability of the shareholder is limited to the value of the share he is purchasing. If the share has been fully paid for then the shareholder has nothing more to pay, even if the company goes broke owing millions of pounds.

A debt/equity ratio that is greater than 100 per cent indicates that the lenders are lending more to the company than the shareholders have put in. Lenders will normally require considerable security if they even approach that situation and the shareholders could rapidly find that everything they own is 'in hock' to the bank (ie the lenders have a charge over all the assets and have the power to march in and seize them if the company defaults on their agreement in any way).

In 20XX, a debt/equity of 250 per cent would be an indicator of serious financial problems. While there is no hard and fast rule and every case must be considered on its merits (or lack of them) it is usually true that a debt/equity of more than 60 per cent causes the lenders a great deal of anxiety.

The imposition of sound cash management in Nephew Ltd would seem to have come just in time. Without it, there might have been a limit to the bank's patience and who knows what the result of that would have been?

Interest Cover	2.5	–

The level of interest cover that is considered to be acceptable varies greatly depending on the type of trade and the security that has been offered to the lenders of finance. Generally, most people wish to be sure that if there is a downturn in trade then the interest payments can still be paid, so investors are looking for quite high interest cover ratios in volatile companies, or those in trades that are subject to rapid peaks and troughs. 20XX would have caused considerable anxiety but the sound cash management noted above has eradicated any problems in 20X1.

Profit management

Return on Capital Employed	48.5%	50.4%

We are looking for a return on capital employed that is higher than the highest cost of interest that the company is paying. The company is paying 18 per cent interest on overdraft but is earning an excellent 48.5 per cent in 20XX on the capital employed, and 50.4 per cent in 20X1.

This excellent performance in 'bottom-line' management

emphasizes the tragedy that would occur (and does occur in real life) if the company was forced into liquidation because of such appalling cash management in 20XX.

Gross Profit %	25.5%	24.7%

The level of gross profit percentage depends on the type of industry and the way the company is being run. It is a key ratio and if many companies turned their attention to the improvement of this and three or four other ratios then very often the ROS (return on sales) would look after itself.

When examining trends, this ratio should be increasing, but in the case of Nephew Ltd a management decision was made to sacrifice a little profit in return for a lot of cash (which was urgently needed at the time to stave off liquidation). As a result, assets were sold and leased back with the subsequent charge at a slightly higher rate than the depreciation that had formerly been charged.

OPERATING MARGIN (ROS)	9.8%	8.0%

The return on sales (operating margin) is the number-one indicator for many companies and it influences most of their management decision-making. In Nephew Ltd, it has fallen over the two years and there are a number of companies' management teams that would go into spasm at this news. All sorts of economies would be looked for and managers would rush all over the place to 'right this wrong'. Senior managers would begin to look long-faced and mutter darkly, with the all-time favourites being: 'We must do something before disaster strikes... we must cut overheads... look for more productivity... look for short-time working... hold down pay increases... begin to lay off staff if we can't reverse this trend.'

Nearly all such thinking is way off the mark because it ignores the fact that profit is made by the level of activity times the operating margin.

Thus, if you increase the level of activity and sell more then you can afford to shave the ROS and still make more profit. For example:

- Sales of £100,000 at a ROS of 12% results in an operating profit of £12,000.
- Sales of £200,000 at a ROS of 10% results in an operating profit of £20,000.

Which level of operating profit would you rather have: £12,000 or £20,000?

It is not the ROS that is important but the activity times the ratio. This is never better illustrated than by Nephew Ltd where the ROS ratio has moved significantly adversely from 9.8 per cent to 8.0 per cent and yet operating profits have risen by £60,000 and after-tax profits by £57,100.

The operating margin (ROS) has a place in management ratios but only when considered in conjunction with others.

Overheads %	61.5%	67.4%

Overheads are incurred simply to increase the gross profit by a greater sum than the cost of the overhead. Otherwise, don't incur the overhead.

This is again a most obvious statement and most people who start a business with their own cash recognize it only too rapidly. Unfortunately, as businesses get bigger and more departments get added that are further away from the 'sharp end' of selling and producing, so the daily task often becomes an end in itself. Jobs come into being, and must be completed, whether or not there is any beneficial effect on the profit.

It is true to say that many managers give their all to completing the daily tasks that are demanded of them by their employers, often working many more than the 35 hours mentioned in their contracts. The demands of their daily tasks leave very little time for them to consider the effects of their actions on the cash management and profit management of the business. The main struggle is to complete the daily task, whatever that might be.

It is in this environment that costs often rise out of all proportion to the benefits that the company receives, and the overheads percentage is a good way of measuring and keeping these costs under control.

The overheads percentage is showing a rise in Nephew Ltd and should be watched carefully to ensure it doesn't keep moving in this direction without substantial benefits to the operating and after-tax profits.

Stock Turnover	17.9	36.2

See the comments under stock days in the cash management section above.

Asset Turnover	2.1	3.5

The accountant of a company is usually inundated with requests for cash from all parts of the company. Some managers need cash to repair and maintain the premises or plant, some to buy new. Others need it to generate or promote a product in existing or new markets, some to lease or buy new offices and so on.

There are methods that accountants use to measure these requests. Many of the requests will result in increased sales throughput and very possibly increased 'bottom-line' profits (operating profit or after-tax profit). However, some of this apparent profit improvement might have come about simply because the depreciation charges are less than the cost of leasing, and thus you are getting 'accountants' profits' rather than any genuine improvement in performance.

Similarly, an acquisition will improve the level of sales and profits simply by consolidating the profit and loss figures of the acquired company in with your own. Earnings per share will increase but, again, there may have been no improvement in the performance of the company.

In the late twentieth century, the ability to write off goodwill immediately from the consolidated balance sheet and the reserves of the company further distorted performance, but such write-offs can be traced in most annual accounts. If you add back the goodwill write-off, and any adjustments for 'fair value' (or any other adjustments you learn about) then you have a better measure of performance. The asset turnover is a good indicator of whether any improvement has come from the performance of the company in the year or from 'buying in' more 'bottom line'.

In the case of Nephew Ltd it can be seen that the asset turnover is increasing, indicating that the growth in sales has come from existing assets (organic growth is still the 'in-phrase' for internal growth).

Revenue per Unit	£9.60	£9.60
Gross Profit per Unit	£2.45	£2.37
Operating Profit per Unit	£0.94	£0.77

These three ratios would tell us more if the unit were significant. In Nephew Ltd we have taken the unit as a unit of production and thus there is a marginal (3 per cent) slippage at gross profit per unit with an 18 per cent slippage in operating profit per unit. There has, however, been a significant increase in volume (100,000 units to 200,000 units) and both these ratios need to be looked at with the volume of throughput in mind.

Personnel ratios

	£(000)s	
Sales per Capita	£160.00	£174.55
Gross Profit per Capita	£40.80	£43.09

Throughput is 100 per cent up in 20X1 but the number employed has increased by a lower percentage (83 per cent), so we see an improvement in these ratios. The increase in gross profit per capita would indicate that the cost of the extra staff has been adequately covered by the increased performance.

Operating Profit per Capita	£15.73	£14.04

The slippage in this ratio needs to be carefully monitored to ensure that it is not the start of a trend that will eventually result in the erosion of Nephew Ltd's profits.

Employee Costs per Capita	£9.50	£11.55

A dramatic increase per capita would be an indication that there has been a large pay award in the year or that more highly paid employees have been recruited, or both. In the case of Nephew Ltd we know that it is the recruitment of the sales staff at a salary much higher than that paid to others that has caused this increase.

Employee costs per capita will need to be closely monitored to ensure that gross profit and operating profit per capita move in the same direction and that the increase in employees' costs is fully absorbed by the increased performance of the company.

Overheads per Capita	£25.10	£29.05

Overheads are moving upward faster than the number of full-time equivalent employees. As overheads are usually incurred to improve profits then any disproportionate increase should be avoided. An increase in this ratio can indicate a move away from labour-intensive support into equipment-intensive support (eg the increasing movement to computer-based systems and solutions may result in increased costs of running the systems while fewer direct workers are needed to support the operations).

Units per Capita	16.66	18.18

This is often taken to be a measure of productivity, either with all the full-time equivalent employees used or just the direct employees.

In the ratio for Nephew Ltd, the effects of doubling the throughput from the 83 per cent increase in the number of employees can be clearly seen in this ratio.

Indirect Ratio	2.0	2.7

The movement away from direct workers and towards support staff that is common in many companies is clearly seen in the indirect ratio of Nephew Ltd.

Capital Employed per Capita	£32.43	£27.85

In 20X1, the amount of shareholders' funds committed to non-working capital and fixed assets has increased less than the number of full-time employees.

Shareholders' Ratios		
earnings per share (eps)	41p	90p

The dramatic increase in earnings per share, along with the improvements in debt/equity, interest cover, return on capital employed and the other shareholders' ratios shown below, must make the shareholders of Nephew Ltd deliriously happy.

Price/Earnings (p/e)	6.1	8.7

The market price per share (obtainable from the daily newspapers for companies that are quoted on the stock exchange) has increased dramatically for Nephew Ltd (from £2.50 to £7.80) and a p/e of 8.7 would indicate that the improved performance is expected to be sustained over the next few years. If there was an expectation of a continued surge upward in profits over the following years then the p/e would have increased yet further and it would be showing above the industry's norm.

Dividend Yield	4.0%	2.3%

If the dividend yield policy is continued then this trend, along with that shown by the dividend cover, indicates the type of company that would be expected to give high capital gains (ie share price increases) rather than increases in income. With only 2.3 per cent in dividends on the money spent on the shares, your money is returning a much lower income than that available from a bank or building society. The share price is increasing, however, and if you were able to sell your shares on the market without effecting the price then the original investor would have seen their shares grow from £1 a share of original investment to £7.80 a share two years later.

Dividend Cover	4.1	5.0

The increase in dividend cover indicates that a greater proportion of the earnings have been retained by the company in 20X1 than in the previous year. The shareholder would thus be looking for the management of the company to use this money to further increase profits and provide increased capital gain through the increased valuation of their shares.

As an example of capital gain, if you had bought the 20,000 shares when offered at the end of 20XX for £50,000 (£2.50 each) then over the 12 months of 20X1 they would have earned you £106,000. If they were publicly quoted and your disposal was not significant enough to disturb the market (remember when shares, like apples, are plentiful and there are loads to sell then the price falls) then you could have sold them a year later at £7.80 a share. This would give you a capital gain of £5.30 (£7.80 – £2.50) a share. If you multiply that figure by the number of shares you held (20,000) it equals £106,000 and you would have more than doubled your money in that year.

If you sold them 'ex-div' (after the dividend had been declared) then you could have received another £3,600 in dividends in that year. Not bad if you can get it! If you sold your share 'cum div', the final dividend goes to whoever bought the shares from you.

What does it all mean? What actions should these ratios provoke? What would your overall reactions be if you were a director of Nephew Ltd and what would your future actions be?

You should have a feeling of great joy if the company achieves all it has forecast for 20X1 – and the ratios give you a veritable tool chest to help you achieve them.

Using the Nephew ratios

Keep an eye on the debtor days, creditor days and stock days and make sure they don't slip backwards after all the improvements.

Reduce the non-working capital and acid test ratios, preferably by using the funds in the business where they can make high returns on the capital employed instead of leaving them sitting in the bank earning very little.

With no debt and high cash holdings, the company is in an excellent position to look for an acquisition that will fit well with the existing expertise. (Remember the warning that very few acquisitions actually work in real life despite all the wonderful prospects when the takeover is in process.) Be sure that you have worked out precisely where the return on the money spent on the acquisition is going to come from and then carefully monitor it to ensure that it really materializes. Produce a set of management accounts that does not write off goodwill.

Keep an eye on the gross profit percentage to ensure that it is maintained at or about 25 per cent and see if the overheads percentage can be returned to or below 62 per cent of the gross profit.

Keep the asset turnover moving upward, thus restricting the 'buying of the bottom line' at a price on which you can never make an adequate return.

Keep an eye on the gross profit per unit to ensure that no further deterioration takes place.

An eye on the per capita ratios should ensure that the company avoids employing people who are not contributing to the profitability and that employee costs are not increasing out of hand.

And that's about it. You can see from the above that ratios act as a guide, a friend of the manager that allows him or her to keep a finger on the pulse of the company without having to investigate every single figure or transaction. They are in many ways comparable to the instruments of the flight deck of the modem aircraft.

The pilot of the modem aircraft does not have to correct the trim of the aircraft every second of every flight, otherwise there would be some very sick passengers being pitched all over the place. Rather he continually monitors the instruments and makes a correction when one or more of them begins to disclose that some action is needed from the pilot. So it is with ratios.

If a ratio starts to deteriorate then keep an eye on it and once action is deemed to be necessary to correct it then it should be implemented without delay. The nature of the ratio should indicate what type of action is necessary or what part of the business to look at. Once the ratio is back within the target levels then the pressure can come off that part of the business and attention be given to other management tasks.

The ratios are also the 'alarm bells' that ring on the flight deck of the company when something is drastically wrong and then they are ignored at the pilot's peril, whether that pilot be you, the managing director, the accountant or any other interested party.

If companies would only produce 'unadjusted' management accounts that could be relied on to be almost accurate, and their managers learn to use the significant ratios for control, then many companies would be far more successful. They would have time to concentrate the available management skills on the part of the business that really needs it rather than have numerous meetings from which they gallop off in all directions at once as is so often seen when crisis threatens.

There is an almost macho image about the manager working late into the night in some mistaken belief that it is the quantity of the hours put in that matters rather than the quality of what is achieved in those hours. Sixty hours a week going round in circles is a poor alternative to 35 hours focused on the real needs of the company.

If you have read through to here then, in the earlier chapters, you have proved that you are capable of understanding business accounts and, in this chapter, you have developed your skills to include the assessment of all the strengths and weaknesses of a company. As with all skills, however, they need practice to get to any real level of competence.

If you really want to master finance then practice makes perfect. By getting this far you may well have learnt as much as you need and I would be delighted if that were so. On the other hand, you may wish to develop your knowledge further and I do encourage you to work out ratios on any other sets of accounts you can lay your hands on, including those in this book. Work out the ratios and see what tales they tell.

You could also get hold of the published accounts from a number of companies (this can often be done by writing to their registered office with a request for them). Then learn all you can from them by reading the report, studying the accounts and calculating the ratios. Determine what actions you believe the company needs to take over the forthcoming years.

If you can achieve even half of the above suggestions then you are truly well on the way to understanding business accounts.

Remember it takes an accountant five years to qualify, so you need a little more than this book, but *How to Master Finance* should have given you a sound understanding of the mechanics that lie behind the accounting reports and some of the terms used by accountants. It should also have left you with a sound understanding of the logic of finance and, I hope, sound principles on which to found your future financial actions.

It's time for you to reflect on how far we've journeyed together since you turned the first pages of this book. I sincerely hope that you've enjoyed reading it and gained some knowledge from it. I have certainly enjoyed putting it together.

Finally, as a little teaser, I couldn't resist reproducing an extract of a set of accounts that could well be a company from the food industry, or electronics, or textiles, or the leisure industry, or pharmaceuticals, or even a combination of them all. I've given you their balance sheet and profit and loss account for the years 20XX, 20X1, 20X2, and 20X3.

I hope you are at the stage where you cannot wait to try out your new skills of financial analysis and complete all the ratios on 'Terry's teaser' and then sit down to decide whether you would invest in the company.

I've left it for you to take out the performance ratios and decide if you would have put all your money in this company or not. It could be a high flyer or a financial disaster – you choose! Have fun and judge for yourself.

Terry's teaser

PROFIT AND LOSS Account

For the Year £000s	20XX	20X1	20X2	20X3
SALES	273.7	380.8	967.1	1,162.0
Less COST OF SALES	(175.3)	(244.9)	(707.5)	(866.1)
GROSS PROFIT	98.4	135.9	259.6	295.9
Less OVERHEADS				
Distribution Costs	(6.9)	(13.5)	(27.9)	(47.1)
Administration	(15.5)	(28.9)	(85.0)	(109.9)
Other Operating Income	0.5	0.8	10.2	9.3
	(21.9)	(41.6)	(102.7)	(147.7)
OPERATING PROFIT	76.5	94.3	156.9	148.2
Interest	(6.5)	(9.6)	(12.8)	12.5
PRE-TAX PROFITS	70.0	84.7	144.1	160.7
Taxation	(9.0)	(16.5)	(26.3)	(22.6)
AFTER-TAX PROFITS	61.0	68.2	117.8	138.1
Dividends	(7.3)	(11.8)	(26.0)	(49.3)
Retained Profits for the Year	53.7	56.4	91.8	88.8
Employed (000s)	3.456	5.283	13.630	17.222

Terry's Teaser
BALANCE SHEET as at year end

As at Year End £(000)	20XX	20X1	20X2	20x3
FIXED ASSETS				
Land & Buildings	128.1	187.6	385.6	734.2
Plant & Equipment	29.7	27.6	119.8	189.3
Vehicles & Other	–	6.0	9.4	92.3
	157.8	221.2	514.8	1,015.8
INVESTMENTS	3.9	1.3	4.8	18.3
INTANGIBLE ASSETS	–	–	–	335.6
CURRENT ASSETS				
Stock	35.8	68.4	128.1	246.5
Debtors	110.1	154.4	196.6	443.7
Cash & Short-term	18.1	20.6	124.2	249.3
Total Current Assets	164.0	243.4	448.9	939.5
CURRENT LIABILITIES				
Creditors	40.1	61.7	147.6	279.5
Borrowings	37.9	42.7	85.5	388.7
Taxation	14.8	20.3	24.8	42.2
Dividends	7.3	11.8	21.8	49.3
Total Current Liabilities	100.1	136.5	279.7	759.7
NET CURRENT ASSETS	63.9	106.9	169.2	179.8
Total CAPITAL EMPLOYED	225.6	329.4	688.8	1,549.5
LONG-TERM LIABILITIES				
Loans	61.7	132.2	302.6	705.8
NET ASSET VALUE	163.9	197.2	386.2	843.7
SHAREHOLDERS' FUNDS				
Ordinary Share Capital	10.9	14.3	24.4	37.8
Preference Capital	1.3	1.3	0.7	0.7
Revaluation Reserve	53.1	89.5	148.1	254.8
Share Premium Reserve	25.8	47.8	186.9	478.7
Revenue Reserve	72.8	44.3	26.1	71.7
TOTAL Shareholders' Funds	163.9	197.2	386.2	843.7

Glossary

accountants' profits   By 'taking a view' of certain transactions and/or asset values and their depreciation, and/or adjusting some values in the accounts, the accountant is able to produce a profit and loss account that shows profits that have not been earned by the company!

Accounting Standards Board (ASB)   A body of people charged with the task of setting standard accounting interpretations and treatment for items that appear in accounts.

annual general meeting (AGM)   A meeting of the members (shareholders) of a company at which the board of directors lay the company's accounts and report for shareholders' approval. Other business is also conducted such as election of directors, auditors remuneration, etc.

annual report and accounts   Most organizations are required to produce an annual report on their activities and enclose the accounts of the company's performance over the past year.

auditors   Professional accountants who check the books of account, ask for explanations from the directors and examine the report and accounts, verifying that they give 'a true and fair view' of the transactions.

bad debt   The amount owed by a customer who cannot, or will not, pay for goods or services they have had. Bad debts can be mitigated if the advice shown under debtor days in this book is followed.

balance sheet   A list of all we own and all we owe.

balancing allowance   This occurs where an asset is sold at a price below that used by the taxman in calculating that asset's written-down value after the company's use of annual capital allowances.

balancing charge   This occurs where an asset is sold at a price above that used by the taxman in calculating that asset's written-down value after the company's use of annual capital allowances.

bank rate   In the UK it is set by the Bank of England, apparently to control the money supply and inflation. Banks usually lend at anything from 2 per cent above bank rate and upward (sometimes rapidly upward), and pay 2 to 3 per cent below bank rate on any deposits you have at the bank.

board of directors   A group of people to whom the shareholders have delegated the task of running the day-to-day affairs of the company. They normally define the direction of the company and thus should have a dramatic influence on its performance. They are supposed to act in the best interest of the shareholders.

bond   A form of IOU issued by the company, or a government or other institution, offering to pay interest in return for borrowing your money, or to pay you little or no interest but instead issue the bonds at a discount but pay you back in full sometime in the future, or to pay you back at some time in the future in a way that is financially interesting to you now.

book value   The value at which an asset stands in the books of the company. It is usually the original cost, plus any increase for revaluation, less any amounts that have been written off profits by way of depreciation etc.

budget   A forecast for a period ahead that becomes the financial embodiment of the company's strategy.

capital employed Sometimes called total assets less current liabilities or total shareholders' funds plus long-term finance (the two calculations provide the same result). It is a measure of how much value is placed in the hands of the management of the company, hence ROCE (return on capital employed) is a key ratio in the control of performance.

charge over assets Used when all or some of the assets of an organization have been used as collateral to secure a tran-saction of some kind (usually the borrowing of large sums of money). The charge operates in a similar way to that used by mortgage companies as they retain an interest in your house and must be repaid first out of any sale monies you make.

collateral Security, usually for a loan. It is effected by enabling the giver of the loan the right to seize the asset that is being used as collateral and sell it if the terms of their loan are not met. See also charge over assets.

company's report and accounts See also annual report and accounts.

consolidated accounts Are set up to provide relevant informa-tion about the economic activities of enterprises that are working together in a group. The results, assets and liabilities of the enter-prises, are aggregated on the basis that they all form part of a single economic unit.

contribution The value that results when all the variable costs are deducted from the sales value of a product, or for a company or division.

cost of goods sold A subtotal on the accounts of the 'direct costs' of the purchase and production of the goods that were sold (ie materials, direct labour, direct expenses and, where appro-priate, this sub-total usually includes the factory costs).

cost of production Similar to cost of goods sold and used mostly in academic accounts.

cost of sales Sometimes used in place of cost of goods sold, particularly in service industries.

creative accounting See accountants' profits.

creditor days The average number of days taken to pay suppliers.

creditors Suppliers to whom we owe money.

creditors, non-trade People to whom we owe money who are not suppliers of products or services within the normal type of trade, eg money owed on loans, to tax authorities, etc.

current ratio Current (short-term) assets as a ratio to current (short-term) liabilities; in days before cash management took over from traditional accounting practices it was known as the 2:~1 ratio.

customer credit days See debtor days.

debentures A type of loan.

debt/equity The proportion of borrowings to shareholders' funds.

debtor days The average number of days the debtors (customers) are taking to pay their accounts.

debtors The amount outstanding on customers' accounts.

debtors, non-trade People who owe us money who are not customers within the normal type of trade, eg money in associated companies, or loaned to somebody, etc.

depreciation The value of the write-down of an asset to allow for the costs of wear and tear over a period of time.

direct costs Costs associated with or comprising part of the actual products or services, eg direct materials, direct labour, direct expenses, etc.

direct labour   The cost of the labour force who worked on the actual products or services.

director   A member of the board of directors who bears the responsibility of managing the company on behalf of the shareholders.

dividend per share   The total dividends paid and proposed by the company and shown as distributed (paid or to be paid) from after-tax profits on the profit and loss account. The total is divided by the number of shares that have been issued in the class of share for which the dividend has been declared.

dividends   The amount of cash paid to shareholders as their share of the distributed profits.

earnings   A phrase that is often interchangeable with profits.

FIFO   'First in first out': an inventory (stock) costing system whereby the items are charged out of stock and into production on the basis that the item that has been longest in stock is the first one out into production. In days of rapidly changing stock values FIFO would give a different value for the production of the period than LIFO (see below).

fixed assets   Assets that you intend to keep for longer than twelve months.

fixed costs   Costs that vary over time rather than in proportion to throughput, eg rent of premises, salaries, etc.

GAAP   Generally approved accountancy practices.

gearing   The proportion of borrowings to total financing (ie shareholders' funds plus total borrowings).

IASC   International Accounting Standards Committee.

indirect costs   Costs that are not directly involved in the making of the product, eg office costs, the cost of receptionists or accounting, etc.

insolvent A company is insolvent when the total value of its liabilities exceeds the total value of its assets.

interest The income from a bank or other financial institution on money you have on deposit, and/or the amount you have been charged on borrowings you have from them.

inventory Used instead of the term stocks to describe the value of the items in the warehouse, on the shop-floor, or in the finished goods department.

just-in-time (JIT) A stock-control system whereby goods are ordered to arrive at the factory just in time before the last item of stock runs out. An efficient JIT system can generate huge amounts of cash formerly tied up in inventory and cause a dramatic improvement in production methods. An inefficient JIT system can cause chaos, loss of production and earn itself a nickname of 'just too bloody late' stock-control system.

LIFO 'Last in first out': an inventory (stock) costing system whereby the items are charged out of stock and into production on the basis that the item that has just been received is the first one out into production. One hopes that the business uses the old stock first but as far as the costings go the old stock stays on the shelf. In days of rapidly changing stock values LIFO would give a different value for the production of the period than FIFO (see above).

liabilities Amounts we owe.

liquidator A person, often an accountant, who specializes in going into companies with a view to realizing cash on their assets, even if it means selling them off and closing down the company.

long-term liabilities Borrowings on which the final date of repayment is more than twelve months ahead.

management buyout (MBO) The management of a company buy that company, or part of it, from its owners. (Most MBOs mysteriously generate far more profits and cash than they did under someone else's ownership!)

manufacturing accounts   The layout of a set of accounts for a manufacturing company that is beloved by theorists and the stuff of many exam curricula. They are hardly, if ever, found in practice.

market capitalization   The stock-market value of a company. It is calculated by multiplying the total number of issued ordinary shares by today's price per share as quoted on the stock market.

medium-term liabilities   Similar to long-term liabilities but the final repayment date is approximately 1 to 5 years away.

members   The shareholders of a company.

minority interests   The value that is attributable to the owners of shares (other than those in the ownership of the parent group) in one or more of the subsidiary companies that form the group.

Nephew Ltd   The company that John Nephew and his wife formed with their inheritance.

off-balance sheet   Arrangements that allowed companies to hold assets or liabilities in such a way that they do not appear on the balance sheet, and thus the true value of the items may not be disclosed in the accounts. (What happened about the 'true and fair view' did I hear you ask? Ah well, accountants are continually dreaming up ways of making the balance sheet and profit and loss account look better and somehow get around that phrase that has stood for years as a way of giving interested parties confidence in the accuracy of the accounts!)

PBIT   Profit before interest and tax.

payments in advance   The total amount of payments we have made when we have paid some bills in advance of receiving the goods or services is listed amongst debtors (people who owe us money or, in this case, the value of goods and services we have paid for).

prime costs A refinement of direct costs that describes the expenditure incurred directly on the product, eg materials, direct labour, direct expenses, etc. It is more often used in academic and theoretic accounts than in practice, and thus not included in this book where the more popular description of direct costs is used.

provision An amount that is shown as an expense in a profit and loss account to cover possible future liabilities, eg provision for bad debts. The same amount is listed on the balance sheet as a liability (in the case of provision for bad debts, it is deducted from the debtor figure shown in current assets). By using a provision the profit is reduced but no cash is involved or set on one side.

prudence An accounting convention that encourages the accountant to take the pessimistic view rather than the optimistic. Most accountants regularly embrace prudence until the chief executive requires more profit from the 'figures'.

Public Limited Company (PLC or plc) A company that invites the public to subscribe for its shares, or securities, or whose shares are quoted on a stock exchange and traded.

receiver A receiver is put into a company to recover a specific debt owed to the people who put him in (see also liquidator).

report and accounts See annual report and accounts.

return on capital employed (ROCE) This ratio is arguably the most vital for the control of performance in large, delegated, businesses. It is made up from the comparison of the PBIT and the capital employed in the business. Put simply, every £1 of value put into the company must produce a yield higher than that obtainable from holding your money on deposit somewhere, and commensurate with the risk the investors face. If the organization is borrowing money then the ROCE needs to be a lot higher than the cost of the borrowed money; if it isn't then don't borrow the money! It is a measure of the performance of the company's management.

return on investment (ROI) A measure of the return on the investment made by the shareholders in the organization. Clearly it must be above that obtainable from similar investment placed on deposit and be commensurate with risk.

ROS   Return on sales.

revenue   A term usually used to depict sales income.

revenue reserve   It might be called a reserve but there is nothing tangible there!

SORPS   Statement of recommended practices.

SSAP   Statement of standard accounting practice. These are guidelines to accountants instructing them on the accounting treatment of various items.

sales   The title given to the value of the invoiced and cash sales a company has made (not the value of the cash collected from the customers!).

sales mix   The mix of different products and/or services that were sold in a given period.

securities   Government bonds, ordinary shares in companies, debentures, loans, preference shares, etc. are all collectively described as securities.

security   Often demanded by banks and other lenders of money as collateral for their loan. This usually involves them taking a charge over some or all of the company's assets (and if that is not enough to cover the borrowings then they will also try for a charge over the personal assets of its owners).

shareholders' funds   The value of the shareholders' investment made up from the nominal value of their shares plus the amount of retained profits and any capital reserves or profits that have been retained.

shares at par or nominal value   The shares are valued at the price shown on the share certificate rather than the price they are trading at in the stock market that day.

short-term assets   Usually called current assets. These are assets that have been purchased with the intention of turning them back into cash within the following twelve months.

short-term liabilities   Called current liabilities. These are debts that we expect to repay over the following twelve months.

solvency   When total assets exceed total liabilities, the reverse of insolvency.

stock   Used to describe the value of the items in the warehouse, on the shop floor, or in the finished-goods department.

stock control   In the days of massive factories and production-led companies, stock control was used to describe the system employed to manage the stock in the warehouse and the stores, to transfer it into production and on to finished stocks until it was sold and sent out to the customer. In the modern market-led companies, the stock-control systems transfer items through the system on a JIT basis.

stock days   The average number of days that products stay in stock before being assembled and or sold.

stock exchange   See stock market.

stock market   The title given to the market that trades in company shares.

suppliers' credit days   More often called creditor days or supplier days, or even purchases days; see creditor days.

trading account   The layout of a set of accounts for a trading company that is beloved by theorists and the stuff of many exam curricula. They are hardly ever found in practice.

trading profit   Sometimes called operating profit, it is usually the profit before investment activities, interest and tax.

true and fair view   Most auditors sign the annual accounts as giving a 'true and fair view' of the transactions of the company over the period covered by the report. Occasionally, some 'qualify' their report with any reservations they may have but the number of unqualified reports that are attached to liquidated companies – often where disaster was occurring during the years of 'clean' auditors' reports – show just how much of an inexact science this is.

turnover   Another title for the value of sales or revenue (but also used in discussing the turnover of stock or assets, etc.).

variable costs   Costs that vary in some kind of proportion to throughput (production), eg materials. Each same product takes the same amount of material, so there is a direct proportion between the number of products produced and the amount of material that was used.

value added tax (VAT)   The European equivalent to sales tax. The company or person selling the service or product charges the customer a tax (VAT) and passes it on to the government's tax collector once they have deducted the VAT they paid on their own qualifying purchases.

winding-up   The work of liquidators and receivers.

work in progress   As its name implies, it is the value of the products on which work has been started but is not yet complete.

working capital   Known to everyone who has attended a Terry Gasking seminar in the last 10 years as non-working capital. It is the total of an organization's short-term (current) assets less its short-term (current) liabilities, and it certainly does not work for you!

write down   The reduction in value of an asset.

writing down allowance   A tax allowance against the costs of an asset.

Index